# Wentworth by the Sea

## The Life and Times of a Grand Hotel

# Wentworth by the Sea

## The Life and Times of a Grand Hotel

J. Dennis Robinson

Peter E. Randall Publisher
Portsmouth, New Hampshire
2004

© 2004 by Ocean Properties Ltd.
Printed in Hong Kong

Book Design: Grace Peirce, J. Dennis Robinson
Jacket Design: Grace Peirce

Peter E. Randall Publisher, LLC
Box 4726, Portsmouth, NH 03802
www.perpublisher.com

Distributed by
University Press of New England
Hanover and London

Library of Congress Control Number: 2003114423

ISBN 1-931807-21-3

FRONT END LEAF: Bird's eye view poster, c. 1883, of "The Wentworth, New Castle, N.H., Frank Jones, Proprietor, Geo. F. Thompson, Manager." Drawn by R. Caughey, Del. Published by Forbes Co., Boston. Photograph courtesy of Bill Truslow, poster from private collection.

REAR END LEAF: Aerial view of the new Wentworth by the Sea. Photograph courtesy Ocean Properties Ltd.

JACKET COVER: Lithograph, n.d. of "The Wentworth." As first remodeled by Frank Jones. Published by Russell and Richardson Co., Boston. Portsmouth Athenaeum Collection.

# DEDICATION

To my parents, Phyllis and John,
who have been waiting fifty years
for me to write a real book

# ACKNOWLEDGMENTS

In 1995, years before this project began, Maryellen Burke arrived in Portsmouth, New Hampshire, and was hired by the Friends of the Wentworth (FOW). At the Portsmouth Athenaeum, she organized and cataloged the extensive collection of images and papers donated by Wentworth by the Sea owners James and Margaret Smith. Later she suggested that I run some of the information on my Web site. Little did I know that she would become my wife. Little did she know that she would be my key support on this book—sharing every day of its writing for a full year. For her tireless editing, reading aloud, suggestions, patience, and wisdom—I could never thank her enough.

After commissioning this work, Ocean Properties offered the greatest gift a writer can have—free rein to tell the whole story. Special thanks to Wentworth by the Sea owner Billy Walsh, manager Tom Varley, and public relations manager Stephanie Seacord. For rebuilding Wentworth by the Sea, I and thousands more thank the Walsh family for their vision and courage in bringing it back.

After saving the Wentworth from destruction, the Friends of the Wentworth fully supported the idea of this history. Without their efforts and vision, this would be a book about a memory, rather than about a thriving hotel. Special thanks to Etoile Holzaepfel for spearheading the causes of the hotel and this volume, and thanks to FOW former director, Albert Rex and board members Peter Bergh, Ronan Donohoe, Darcy Horgan,

OPPOSITE: *Youthful guests at Wentworth by the Sea offered a wholesome and well-balanced image of the otherwise tumultuous 1960s. (ATH)*

Irene Crosby, Bob DeVore, Tony Barrington, Anne Catell, and Maryellen Burke, and to all the supporters of the Friends who helped fund this publication.

Although we scarcely knew each other, I could never have completed this work on time without the extensive research and insights of the late Raymond Brighton. Ray's detailed unpublished manuscript for a proposed history of the Wentworth provided a solid foundation for this book. I am greatly indebted to him for his study of local newspapers, of early New Castle history, and for timely oral histories he collected in the late 1980s. It is a special pleasure that Peter E. Randall, who published so many of Ray's Portsmouth history books, is now my publisher and my friend.

Images and data for this project seemed to come together almost magnetically, as if drawn to a central place precisely when needed. It began with the archived collections of the Portsmouth Athenaeum, managed by keeper Tom Hardiman and supported by librarian Ursula Wright. Then came the amazing unseen materials on the Campbell family offered by family descendants B. J. Plantero and Alice Wentworth. Boston University architectural historian Richard Candee generously loaned the detailed research and artifacts from his personal Wentworth collection. Collector Lew Karabatsis provided images from his collection and Stephan Gianotti donated rare photographs that he had taken inside the old hotel. Nicole Cloutier was ever helpful with materials from the Portsmouth Public Library, and William A. Jewett connected the genealogical links among the family that originally built the hotel, in 1874.

I am very grateful to those who read this manuscript in various drafts and offered corrections and suggestions—Richard Candee, Richard Winslow, James Garvin, Eugene Morrill, Ursula Wright, Phyllis Robinson, Etoile Holzaepfel, and Irene Crosby.

My sincere thanks to all those who have loaned images and documents or offered tips and guidance. More than fifty people with memories of the Wentworth called or e-mailed to share their personal thoughts and memories, stories enough for many volumes this size. They continue to call week after week. I wish I were able to include all their stories, and hope others will collect and archive this valuable information.

# ƒPONƒORƒ

Special thanks to Ocean Properties Ltd. who kindly joined in partnership with the Friends of the Wentworth to fund this project. Without them, this book would not have been possible.

We are indebted as well to the generosity of the following sponsors:

Robert W. Adams
Anonymous New Castle family
Peter Bergh and Janet Prince
Martha Fuller Clark
Robert W. DeVore
Joan Dwyer
Greater Piscataqua Community Foundation
Étoile Heifner Holzaepfel
P. Darcy Horgan
In loving memory of Henry Chandler Horner
In loving memory of Joseph G. Sawtelle
Barbara K. and Cyrus B. Sweet III
Portsmouth Marine Society
TMS Architects
New Castle Historical Trust Fund of the Greater Piscataqua
  Community Foundation

The Wentworth
By the Sea

Tony Fallon 1992

# Contents

# FOREWORD

Everyone I meet lately has a good story or two about the Wentworth Hotel. Here are mine: As a teacher in the late 1970s I attended a conference at Wentworth by the Sea, then a rambling white elephant decades beyond its prime. The sense of something grand and gone permeated every room. A few years later, as the hotel closed and began its twenty-year hibernation, I interviewed its elderly former owners, Margaret and James Barker Smith, who had purchased the hotel in 1946 and managed it for thirty-four consecutive summers. We spoke over the telephone and my nostalgic feature story filled the front page of a weekly newspaper. Pleased with the article, the couple invited me to a party at their New Castle home just across the bridge at the foot of the hotel grounds. The conversation drifted from golf, to tennis, to yachting, to big bands, to financial investments and hotel management—all topics in which I was wholly unschooled.

"I want to give you a present," Margaret Smith said suddenly.

I followed her tiny frame down the cellar stairs and along a basement corridor to a large built-in closet. Mrs. Smith swung open the doors and examined what had to be a hundred small gift boxes, already wrapped and ribboned. With great purposefulness she selected a small square white box and handed it to me as if it were the Hope diamond.

"Thank you," she said graciously, and I thanked her back as she swung the cabinet doors closed. I followed her upstairs to

OPPOSITE: *Styles clash in this 1960s fashion show in the former Colonial dining room at the Wentworth. Once among the largest and most elegant dining areas in New England, the century-old structure was razed during the hotel's "limbo years." (ATH)*

the party. Inside the box was a solid metal bottlecap opener with a crossed golf club insignia and the words WENTWORTH BY THE SEA hand-painted on the brim. It's the best bottle cap opener I've ever owned.

For much of my adult life, then, the hotel was closed. I watched it fall into disrepair like a time-lapse movie through years of bicycle rides around the scenic eight-mile New Castle "loop" that begins and ends in Portsmouth. The paint peeled. The grounds shrank. The pool closed. Buildings disappeared until only the oldest section, defined by three towers, remained.

In 1999 an editor from the world's largest newspaper, *Yurimi Shimbun,* with ten million readers daily, saw my local history Web site and asked me to show him around Portsmouth. He was particularly interested in the historic sites connected with the Russo-Japanese Treaty of 1905. We visited the museum at the Navy Yard and studied the collection at the Portsmouth Athenaeum, then drove the New Castle loop on a drizzly October day. We stopped the car beneath the hulking wooden hotel shell, surrounded by a metal fence. Plans to renovate the building had stalled again and the project hovered in limbo. Locals were losing hope and the hotel had never looked worse.

"Why doesn't your New Hampshire government do something?" the Japanese editor asked as we sat in his rented car. "Don't they understand the importance of this building to the Japanese people?"

They don't, I said, and made weak excuses for why my home state does so very little to preserve its cultural heritage.

Then suddenly, after twenty years of angst and false starts, the hotel was saved. The Friends of the Wentworth, a nonprofit group formed to preserve the old hotel from destruction, found in Ocean Properties a new owner willing to restore the last standing piece of the original building and to reopen the hotel. The chapters in this book took shape in the final six months of construction, even as the hammers rang out on the highest point on Great Island just as they did back in the nineteenth century. Perhaps I have gone too deeply into the past. You be the judge. But I believe a history of the Wentworth is incomplete without an understanding of the island it occupies.

In mid-May 2003, as this little history was falling into place, the Wentworth reopened in a flurry of last-minute construction. A hundred guests tested the modern luxury rooms with their historic view. The following day, as three hundred elegantly dressed visitors attended a kickoff charity ball in the new banquet hall, my wife Maryellen and I were among the first to sample the hotel cuisine. As the sun set and the lights in the domed ceiling rose, our waitress arrived. We could just see Portsmouth in the distance beyond the darkening Little Harbor. Maryellen studied her menu, then smiled up at our server, but as she tried to speak, only tears came. It was a moment she had dreamed of for years.

This book, then, is a kind of emotional architecture: It is my attempt to quickly frame in—with feeling—the full span of Wentworth by the Sea history from its construction in 1873 until its reopening a hundred and thirty years later. It is not, as many readers might expect, predominately the story of the recent Smith era. Squeezing the Smiths into a single chapter was no easy task, but it had to be done so that the full arc of the hotel's history could be clearly seen. As much as ninety percent of the historical hotel materials archived in the Friends of the Wentworth collection at the Portsmouth Athenaeum relates to the Smiths. There are hundreds of Smith letters, documents, and photographs on file. When I solicited the public for family memories about the Wentworth Hotel, four dozen people responded, and all but three remembered only the Smiths.

One response drilled deep into the mother lode. B. J. Plantero, a descendant of the original builder of the hotel, called my office to see if I would be interested in a few scattered documents and photographs. Her great-grandparents Charles and Sarah Campbell had run a guesthouse behind the Wentworth as early as the 1840s. She still had the original leather-bound guest book from Campbell Cottage in New Castle. The Campbells—with an outside investor—built, owned and managed the hotel starting in 1874, but lost the hotel to bankruptcy just three years later. Their adopted son, B. J.'s grandfather, had later been the hotel night watchman and salvaged a few paper lanterns from the famous 1905 peace treaty negotiations. Oh, by the way, B. J.

said, her cousin Alice Wentworth, another Campbell descendant, had even more items.

On a freezing February evening my wife and I sat in Alice's cozy new Portsmouth kitchen. Every square foot of counter space was covered with surprising documents and photographs. Among them we saw, for the first time, young Charles Campbell, a handsome man with a handlebar mustache, and his wife, Sarah, all decked out in furs. Most people connect the face of Portsmouth ale tycoon Frank Jones with the early days of the Wentworth, but the Campbells came first. The hotel on the hill was their idea, it appears, and for the next century, until the Campbells sold the family homestead, the hotel loomed just outside their cottage door.

With the Campbell and Smith historical "bookends" established, there was still a great deal of empty space to fill in the long story of the hotel. The bulk of what follows is drawn largely from hotel marketing brochures and local newspaper accounts. But brochures tell only the owner's side of the story, and newspapers, despite their reputation for recording the unvarnished truth, are often as much propaganda as history. Having written for newspapers since the age of ten, I can verify that.

So this history represents a hotel well timbered, I believe, but only sparsely populated. There are thousands more stories to tell. A portion of the proceeds of this book will go to maintaining the Wentworth by the Sea archive at the Athenaeum. I hope more artifacts and oral histories and exhibits will follow to fill these roughed-out rooms.

To attempt a project of this scope in only a few months, a writer needs to focus. While the structure of the book is chronological, I'm not obsessive about dates. I prefer first to plant the hotel securely in New Castle and then watch the decades race by, picking up speed as we approach the present. I visualized my reader as a guest sitting on the edge of a comfortable bed in the new Wentworth by the Sea hotel. The guest is new to the Piscataqua region and has just returned from a night on the town in nearby Portsmouth. After stopping by the hotel bar, the guest is finally settling in, and dangerously close to tapping the TV remote to find a late-evening movie. Then, for reasons unknown, the guest slides open a drawer beside the bed.

"Hey look," the guest says. "There's a whole book here about this hotel."

"A book about a hotel?" Someone else says, stepping from the shower. "How interesting can that be?"

And if I've done my job, a couple of hours will pass before the TV set blinks on, and that question will be answered. Hotels lead rich and vibrant lives, and this one shows no sign of slowing down.

J. Dennis Robinson

# INTRODUCTION

Wentworth by the Sea is a survivor. It stands though so many other great hotels of its era have disappeared. It did not burn down like most rambling wooden structures lit by gas lamps and crude early electric wires. It did not fall of its own accord. In fact it grew, expanded, and improved until it dominated the high ground of New Castle, New Hampshire. Today's Wentworth by the Sea is not a true reconstruction. A portion of the 1874 building survives within the modernized hotel, to be sure. The front portico and its three towers date to the late 1800s. The large rebuilt wooden mantel in the Roosevelt Room, the old stage in the ballroom, and domed ceiling in what is now the dining room are from that era. But the twenty-first-century Wentworth is reborn, a modern hotel with a rich ancestry. It remains the largest structure on the highest point of a historic island. In many ways Great Island shares as much with its sister Isles of Shoals as it does with the mainland. It was, until the mid-nineteenth century, a sleepy fishing village. Comprising just one square mile, New Castle is the smallest town in New Hampshire, the state with the smallest shoreline of any coastal state in the nation.

So the Wentworth is a very big fish in a very small pond. Though it functions like an independent island, it is linked to the people, to the economy, and to the reputation of the surrounding region. Its history is inseparable from the history of Portsmouth and of the New Hampshire coast. In fact, thanks to

ABOVE: *Ellen McGuirk, at age ninety-five, with owner Margaret Smith. McGuirk first registered at the Wentworth Hotel in 1884. (ATH)*

OPPOSITE: *Young guests enjoy the new Olympic-sized pool as the Victorian hotel approached its centennial in 1973. (ATH)*

the Treaty of Portsmouth, brokered here in 1905, we can safely suggest that the story of the whole world might have played out differently had it not been for what happened at the Wentworth Hotel.

Architecturally, most of the Victorian hotel is lost. Almost seventy percent of the sprawling building was razed as it lay dormant at the end of the twentieth century. Its Colonial Revival detailing and later art deco redesign exist only in photographs. But the essence of the original hotel remains hauntingly the same as the first owners imagined it. A recently rediscovered photograph shows the original hotel exterior as a plain white eighty-foot-long, three-story rectangle poking above the surrounding pines and topped with a boxy little observation room. Actually the hotel was L-shaped to allow commanding water views from every guest window, with an attached wing to house the dining hall and kitchen.

It wasn't until the era of the second owner, Frank Jones, a brewer and a New Hampshire politician, that the familiar turrets were added. Starting around 1880 Jones added a fourth floor and the distinctive red mansard roof that gave the Wentworth its visual identity. It was Jones who transformed the Wentworth into one of the premier luxury hotels on the eastern seaboard and made its reputation. He added the motorized elevators, the electric lights, the flush toilets, and the recreation areas. He doubled the size of the hotel, decorated the ornate public rooms, and even experimented with a hotel of a different color.

In a second burst of costly renovation, toward the turn of the twentieth century, Frank Jones doubled the length of the hotel again. Effectively, he built another hotel alongside the Wentworth and equipped it with a top-floor dining area. Even now it is hard to visualize the extent of Jones's seaside empire, with its cavernous stables, outbuildings, golf links, boat piers, swimming pond, and more. Amazingly, this was only part of the tycoon's unfulfilled dream for an even grander resort.

It seems inevitable that the state's wealthiest nineteenth-century entrepreneur would come to own the Wentworth, a hotel named for Governor Benning Wentworth, New Hampshire's wealthiest and most powerful citizen of the eighteenth century, and whose Colonial mansion is still visible from Wentworth by the Sea today. Future owners, throughout the twentieth century, worked largely within the game plan and the campus defined by Jones. How they adapted his world during the most changeable century in history makes up the second half of this story.

What emerges is a fascinating collection of people and events strung together on the lives of the men, and one woman, who managed Wentworth by the Sea. Their important moments, both failed and successful, give the architecture life. One by one they ran the hive, daily directing hundreds of employees to please hundreds of guests. They managed the buzzing activity in kitchens and stables, on dance floors and tennis courts, in swimming pools and water closets, among yachtsmen and motorists, through fire and hail, amid banquets and masquerade balls.

If there is a lesson embedded in all this, it is a simple one. Hotel people, it appears, run hotels best. Those managers born to the trade, the men with hotel ancestry in their blood, succeeded where others did not. It is thanks to them that Wentworth by the Sea survives, and that its biography is worth telling.

Throughout its long and lucky life, the resilient hotel has been buffeted by New England weather, reduced by flames, threatened by shifting fashions and fickle economics, and shut down by war. It hovered for the longest time in suspended animation with barely a pulse, written off by all but the most dedicated preservationists.

Now Wentworth by the Sea is back, renewed and reopened in the summer of 2003 by Ocean Properties, a family-owned Portsmouth company. Summer 2004 marks the 130th anniversary of the year that David Chase and Charles Campbell opened the boxy Wentworth House to its first guests. Summer 2005 is the centennial of the Treaty of Portsmouth, when Japanese and Russian envoys, while staying at the hotel, negotiated peace to end a war that threatened to engulf Europe and Asia.

It's just one New Hampshire hotel, but it's also a touchstone to the past. It's not a relic or a ruin, but rather a place that once again hums with human activity. It functions today as it did in 1874, but there's more. It functions, too, as a place where we can stand and measure our own lives against the past.

# THE GREAT ISLAND

New Castle feels like no other town in New Hampshire. Visitors sense that immediately. With scarcely a sign, the old road from downtown Portsmouth to New Castle veers off the mainland and leapfrogs onto two small islands, then across a scenic causeway—the roiling dark Piscataqua River on the left, a gentle bay on the right—and onto another island thick with trees. Following a few sharp, slow turns you are in the village, but a village with no stores, no gas station, no sidewalks or central common to speak of. There are no tall buildings, unless you count the lone spire of the Congregational church. The ancient houses huddle together, some just inches from the main road, many decorated with painted wooden plaques proudly proclaiming their construction dates: 1675, 1700, 1725, 1690. If not for the squat white post office and a little white meeting hall, New Castle might be a movie set, a reconstructed colonial fishing village waiting only for a busload of costumed actors to arrive.

In fact, New Castle is the real deal. This unspoiled island village is the ancient heart of New Hampshire. This was the seat of the early colonial government, the nexus of the first British military outpost, and the center of population and commerce by the mid-1600s. Today most people imagine New Castle as a quaint town that survived the hammer of progress because it was situated just outside the city nearby. Actually the story goes the other way. The population center, and with it the industry and

ABOVE: *New Castle village in the 1920s, except for the addition of paved roads, looked very much as it does today. (ATH)*

OPPOSITE: *Great Island was settled by European fishermen in the 1600s. This idyllic illustration by Abbot E. Graves is from the 1884 history of New Castle. (JA)*

government, migrated from the island to the mainland. Portsmouth, the bustling city just upriver, evolved later.

It all makes sense from the air. Hovering above the Piscataqua River, which divides New Hampshire and Maine, the seacoast area appears sparse and fragile. It is. Much of the initial area is wetland, which reflects the sun and seems to belong more to the ocean than the mainland. The spits of white sandy beach between Hampton and Ogunquit are broken up by rocky clumps and cracked by a series of rivers. Ten miles from the Portsmouth harbor, the nine Isles of Shoals, split by the bordering states, scarcely interrupt the sea. Boon Island, off York, Maine, is just an isolated rock hosting New England's tallest lighthouse. The mouth of the Piscataqua is broken by twenty islands, then the tide moves upriver and opens dramatically into a large saltwater bay. The impression, from high above, is that the water dominates and that what land remains is sewn together tenuously by a network of skinny roads and bridges.

Largest of all the coastal islands in New Hampshire is New Castle, but forget that name for a moment. To the original European explorers this was "the great island." It was great not only in size, but in location as well. Positioned at the mouth of the river, it afforded the perfect vantage point from which to defend the entire river valley. Any ship moving up the Piscataqua toward the five key tributaries had to pass the nub of land on Great Island where the settlers immediately built a military fort—and where a fort remains more than 350 years later.

An island is a good place to start a colony, especially if the landmass beyond it is too impossibly large to map, covered in a primal forest of gigantic trees, frigid during long snowy winters, and populated by wild animals and Indian tribes. You need a good reason to come here from Europe in a small wooden ship across thousands of dangerous miles, and you need an extraordinary reason to stay. That reason is money.

Many Americans cling to the theory that this nation grew out of a religious pilgrimage to Massachusetts; however, New Hampshire historians know better. From the start, exploring and colonizing New Hampshire was a business deal. The nation's earliest British land speculators hoped to reap huge profits from

OPPOSITE: *An aerial view of New Castle island shows Kittery, Maine, above, just beyond the Piscataqua River and Rye, New Hampshire, with the golf course below to the south. Portsmouth is to the west. Wentworth by the Sea is near the center just beyond the Little Harbor bridge. Campbell's Island, the summer home of the family who built the Wentworth, is visible just to the left of the hotel. New Castle village is located at the far end of the island and Fort Constitution and Portsmouth Harbor Lighthouse are at the small point of land on the top left. Camp Langdon (now New Castle Common) and Fort Stark are between the lighthouse and the hotel facing east.*
*(ATH)*

New England, originally "Northern Virginia." When no new trade route to China, or precious metals, or even valuable sassafras turned up here, investors settled for what the area had to offer—rich fishing grounds, endless acres of timber, and pelts traded with local Indians.

The evolving early-seventeenth-century fishing community collectively was called "Strawberry Bank." The scattering of homes ran from the Piscataqua through what is now the Portsmouth riverfront as far south as modern-day Rye, then called Sandy Beach. Great Island, in the center, served as the colonial capital. Early New Hampshire explorers marched westward into a primeval forest that, theoretically, extended across the American continent, possibly to China. They got as far as the White Mountains and reported that the new British colony was massive and, except for largely peaceful Indian tribes, unoccupied.

The "corporate" owners of the New Hampshire colony stayed safely in England. In their absence, the colony of Massachusetts slowly assumed protective control during the mid-1600s, when New Castle was the provincial capital.

Strawberry Bank became the town of Portsmouth. New Castle split off as a separate town in 1693 and Rye became a separate parish and later a town in 1785. Each little town, like siblings in a crowded family, developed a unique personality. That would have been the end of the confusion, but nostalgic nineteenth-century Portsmouth historians held fast to the poetic old name. Reviving an early spelling, they referred to the Portsmouth waterfront as "olde Strawbery Banke." In 1823 Portsmouth historians commemorated the 1623 founding date at Rye. The early date, just three years shy of the 1620 founding of Plimouth Plantation in Massachusetts, provided Portsmouth with a claim to rival the Bay State and gave the town a much needed ego boost during poor economic times. The 1823 bicentennial celebration was one of Portsmouth's first attempts to claim and market its history. It cleared the way for what has become the state's second largest industry after manufacturing—tourism.

In 1957, to preserve a few of the many historic buildings being toppled by urban renewal, a nonprofit preservation group established a museum on the Portsmouth waterfront. Built around an early residential area called Puddle Dock, the museum chose instead to revive the name Strawbery Banke, complete with its original spelling. Today the popular museum owns forty early buildings dating from the seventeenth to the nineteenth centuries, including some that were moved to the site. The saltwater puddle has been filled in, and the town's commercial waterfront across the street is now home to Prescott Park, with lush gardens and an outdoor summer theater. Uninitiated tourists and Portsmouth residents naturally assume that the old houses at Strawbery Banke Museum are remnants of the earliest New Hampshire village; in fact, that village is just three miles downriver at New Castle.

Finding no gold, early investors settled on fish, a valuable commodity to Catholic Europe. Even before the evolution of the settlement on Great Island, fishermen from Europe used the nearby Isles of Shoals as their base camp, drying and salting tons of giant cod for export to populations back home. John Smith, of Pocahontas fame, visited the region and named it New England on his famous 1614 map. He also named the nearby Isles of Shoals Smythe Isles, but Smith never returned to found a colony here as he promised, and the name faded.

David Thompson (or Thomson) of Plymouth, England, settled at Rye in 1623 with his wife, Amais, and their son John at what is now Odiorne Point in Rye, New Hampshire. The presumed site of their house at Pannaway Manor is still within view of Wentworth by the Sea. The Thompsons stayed only three years before heading south to a tiny colony called Boston, but other fishermen lingered at the lonely New World outpost. Among them reportedly were the Hiltons, who settled in nearby Dover, also in 1623. Maine settlers at Fort St. George had proved it was possible to survive a single New England winter as early as 1607. But the Hiltons and others showed it was possible to live permanently in the harsh climate. More fishing meant more profit.

Early Wentworth Hotel visitors routinely walked two miles or rowed across the bay to explore the historic founding spot, now part of Odiorne Point State Park. They were drawn to the

TOP: *Matthew R. Thompson's concept of Pannaway Manor in 1623, the first settlement by David Thomson in New Hampshire. The presumed site, at what is now Odiorne's Point in Rye, is just across Little Harbor from the Wentworth. (YAN)*

MIDDLE AND BOTTOM: *New Hampshire cod was dried on racks or "flakes" then transported to Europe where it was highly prized. Fishing and the timber industry, not a desire for religious freedom, provided the impetus that launched the settlement of the Piscataqua region. (JDR)*

ABOVE: *Fort Constitution, formerly Fort William and Mary, as it appeared to visitors in the early twentieth century. The inner wooden buildings no longer survive. (ATH)*

overgrown stone foundations that nineteenth-century writers identified as Mason's Hall, the 1620s-era fishermen's shelter named after John Mason. Mason became owner of the Piscataqua River land granted by the British king when his partner, Ferdinando Gorges, agreed to divide their common holdings, taking Maine for himself.

In his 1884 history of New Castle, John Albee recalls a visit to the hallowed first settlement site, where he saw early gravestones in the ancient cemetery (it still remains today) enclosed by stone walls. Locals had reportedly uncovered a skeleton and left it perched on an old shed, from which the bones had toppled to the ground. Other visitors had tossed artifacts found around the first house ruins into an old wooden box. Disgusted by the scene, Albee wrote:

> So fares it with the Plymouth Rock of New Hampshire. The graves of its heroes neglected, their very bones laying about like broken crockery. And the relics of Mason's Hall consigned to a raisin box! Shame upon the state of New Hampshire! What has she ever done to preserve her early history?

Likely this wasn't the original Mason's Hall, but then, as now, little was done to commemorate the historic spot or to tell the story of New Hampshire's founding family. A granite monument erected to the Thompsons in the last years of the nineteenth century is rarely seen even today. It was moved from its original seaside site and hidden from view near the old cemetery. Albee's complaint against the Granite State is still valid. During World War II the federal government seized the Odiorne family farm to build an elaborate coastal defense system there, further corrupting the site. Now the hulking concrete bunkers of Fort Dearborn have become ruins themselves.

Remnants of a dozen forts line the entrance to the Piscataqua on both the Maine and the New Hampshire sides. Most of the forts were built in the nineteenth and twentieth centuries to defend the Portsmouth Naval Shipyard, established in 1800. The deep, fast-flowing river makes the inner harbor quite easy to defend. From British blockades to marauding German U-

TOP: *John Albee, author of the 1884 history and tour guide of New Castle, reportedly selected the name Wentworth for the hotel. (JA)*

BOTTOM: *A monument to first settler David Thomson at Odiorne Point was erected in the 1899 Colonial Revival era. Today the area is the Seacoast Science Center. (JDR)*

ABOVE: *Forts that dot the Piscataqua River were popular tourist sites in the nineteenth century. Coastal defense enthusiasts believe this image may be from Fort McClary in nearby Kittery, Maine. (BS)*

boats, no enemy has invaded. Only during the early Indian uprisings did residents face an attack. Despite all the forts and guns, no shots from a foreign entity have been fired in battle, with the exception of 1774.

On December 14 of that year, four months before the "shot heard 'round the world" kicked off the American Revolution, New Hampshire patriots raided the fort at New Castle near the fishing village. Although the event rarely makes the history books, the attack on Fort William and Mary—known as the Castle—shocked King George and led swiftly to the end of British rule in New Hampshire. A makeshift militia of four hundred seacoast-area men forced the surrender of just six soldiers stationed at New Castle. The raiders removed about one hundred barrels of the king's precious gunpowder. Shots were fired, but no one was killed and the British group surrendered to the local mob. A larger group returned the next day to steal the cannon and muskets in open defiance of the law.

The raid was spurred by none other than Paul Revere, who made his first warning ride from Boston to alert Portsmouth citizens that the British were coming. In this case, Royal Navy ships were on the way to protect the fort and its ammunition at New Castle from rebellious patriots. They were not coming as quickly as Revere feared, but he managed to incite the locals to riot. By leading the spontaneous little revolution, leaders John Langdon of Portsmouth and John Sullivan of Durham were committing treason, punishable by death. (Both men later became president of the state of New Hampshire.) Months after the raid, the local mob forced royal governor John Wentworth and his family to flee their rented house in Portsmouth and take shelter aboard the British ship *Scarborough,* anchored just off New Castle. Legend says the British commander of the frigate considered laying waste to the rebellious New Hampshire town. Portsmouth dodged this bullet, however, as it has in every armed conflict to date. Instead, John Wentworth and his family escaped on the *Scarborough* to Boston, and as the Revolution erupted, they fled to Halifax, Nova Scotia, never to see their homeland again.

Why this series of events at New Castle does not echo through the halls of American history still mystifies locals. The

ABOVE: *Local militia groups occasionally reenact the attack on Fort William and Mary beginning with the arrival of Paul Revere on a frigid December afternoon.* (RMP)

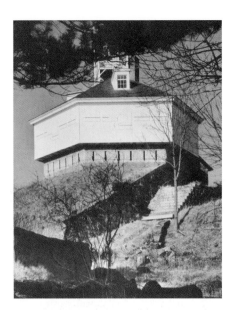

brazen attack and overthrow of the military base there was a key link in the chain that led to the American Revolution, but the raid was apparently not bloody enough for the textbooks. Yet with the ejection of Governor John Wentworth in June 1775, New Hampshire was on its own. Another legend claims that the king's gunpowder stolen from Fort William and Mary made its way to Bunker Hill. There more New Hampshire men served than did militia from any other state—another fact all but lost to history. It wasn't lost, however, on patrons of the Wentworth. Some of the earliest hotel brochures include sketches and photographs of the New Castle fort and the hexagonal Fort McClary, visible across the river in Kittery.

Patriotically renamed Fort Constitution, the Castle was renovated for the war of 1812 and again just before the Civil War. The bloodiest day in New Castle occurred at the fort, ironically, on the Fourth of July in 1809. While preparing for an Independence Day celebration, soldiers planning a patriotic cannon salute left damp gunpowder drying in the sun. Set off by an errant spark, the explosion killed nine men. A severed limb reportedly crashed through the window of a home nearby.

Locals often note that New Castle got its name from the fort that was once more castlelike than it looks today. Town historian Eugene Morrill disagrees with the legend popularized by Albee. He points to evidence that the name was selected in honor of the Duke of New Castle when the town split from Strawberry Bank in the late 1600s. This seems likely, as the names "New England" and "New Hampshire" and the two seacoast counties, Rockingham and Strafford, all pay homage to the British gentry. So too do the names of most surrounding towns, including Durham, Dover, Barrington, Newmarket, Rochester, Somersworth, Exeter, Hampton, Portsmouth, Salem, and Derry.

The fort was newly garrisoned when the concrete Battery Farnsworth, with its disappearing guns, was constructed there between 1897 and 1899. It is minimally maintained by the state of New Hampshire today. Like the first settlement site across Little Harbor in Rye, no significant monument honors the events. Modern tourists are left to wander the nineteenth-century ruins located near the New Castle Coast Guard station.

ABOVE: *The hexagonal Fort McClary is the only fully reconstructed fort along the Piscataqua today. Dating from the Civil War, it stands high above the river on the Kittery, Maine side. The fort is still visible from Wentworth by the Sea. (DA)*

ABOVE: *A view of Fort Constitution and the lighthouse. This perspective was often reproduced as a photo and illustration in Wentworth brochures. (ATH)*

LEFT: *Fort Point, or Portsmouth Harbor Light, took many forms over the years. A taller wooden tower was replaced in the nineteenth century by this shortened light, which greeted the first Wentworth visitors. It was replaced in 1877 by a cast-iron tower that historian John Albee called a "corpulent length of stove pipe." Now painted white, it stands today, and is run by a nonprofit agency. (ATH)*

ABOVE: *Walbach Tower was added quickly to the New Castle fortification around the time of the British blockade in 1814. The ruins were a popular picnic destination for hotel guests. The overgrown brick structure today stands adjacent to the U.S. Coast Guard station. (ATH)*

RIGHT: *Two fashionable visitors pose on the rocks during a trip to the New Hampshire seacoast circa 1890. (ATH)*

The lighthouse adjacent to the fort is the state's only mainland light, in full view of White Island light at the Isles of Shoals and Whaleback Light, which is technically in Kittery, Maine. The Coast Guard has automated all three historic lights and no longer owns or maintains them. New Castle light (also called Fort Point or Portsmouth Harbor light) is a large metal cone, now painted white. A beam has burned at this spot since as early as the 1630s, although it was at first just a light hung on a pole. The current structure was built soon after the hotel opened in 1874. The metal tower was originally painted brown. Historian Albee referred to it as an ugly piece of stovepipe. He preferred the earlier wooden tower, shortened from an eighty-foot lighthouse built there in 1803. That one had replaced the slightly shorter wooden structure built under the orders of poor Governor John Wentworth in 1771. Its beam must have been his last view of his beloved Portsmouth Harbor as he sailed into exile.

Today New Castle's important military history is largely invisible to the casual tourist. Continuing around the New Castle loop road from the village to Wentworth by the Sea are three more fortifications, though none is easy to spot from the road. Hidden among the brush just west of the fort is Walbach Tower, a squat brick structure that looks not unlike a large round cake. Built in 1814, reportedly in a single day during the British blockade of Portsmouth Harbor, it had long gone to ruin by the arrival of the Wentworth Hotel in 1874. It is named for the German-American commander who served forty years at Fort Constitution. Walbach's Castle exerted a strange romantic pull on early hotel visitors, much the way ruins of the Wentworth Hotel drew camera-toting tourists in the late twentieth century. The tower appears on many early postcards and in guidebooks and was the focus of patriotic odes, orations, and summer picnic toasts. Colonel Walbach's widow, still beloved by townspeople in her final years, was treated to a grand Wentworth banquet by hotel owner Frank Jones.

Just up the road at Great Island common, beyond the little sandy beach, is the island's only public recreation site, with picnic areas, a ball field, and a sweeping view of the harbor entrance, where all three lighthouses are visible. For the first half of the twentieth century, locals knew this area simply as the Reservation.

ABOVE: *A contemporary view of Portsmouth Harbor Light at dusk shows Whaleback Light in the distance. Whaleback stands in the middle of the Piscataqua River and is technically in Kittery, Maine. New Hampshire's only offshore light is six miles out to sea at White Island. (HL)*

During World War II the flat, thirty-two-acre spot was renamed Camp Langdon in honor of the Portsmouth patriot who raided the fort nearby. Originally designed for an antiaircraft battery, it was used for training and recruiting during two world wars. Camp Langdon housed a powerful searchlight to spot enemy planes that might threaten the construction of submarines produced at the shipyard. No planes ever did. When the Wentworth suffered its one deadly fire, in 1969, the old military base was converted into dorms for hotel employees.

Closest to the Wentworth, down Wild Rose Lane, are the ruins of Fort Stark, rebuilt again and again on what was another mid-1700s defense site. There are those who argue that this spot, not across Little Harbor at Odiorne's Point, is the site of the first New Hampshire settlement. This military complex, originally called the Battery on Jerry's Point, was going through an active period when the Wentworth opened in 1874, then faded for lack of government funds. Fort Stark was revived at the turn of the twentieth century, again faded during World War I, and was reactivated in 1942, just as Wentworth by the Sea closed for two years of war. Photos of the period show soldiers sitting atop large artillery guns under camouflage tents waiting for action that never came. Today Fort Stark is unmanned and unprotected, a crumbling public park unable to defend itself against an army of vandals.

The town of New Castle was incorporated in 1693 under the reign of King William and Mary. According to an early Wentworth Hotel brochure, the British government was to receive an annual symbolic payment of three peppercorns. Today prime island homes top the million-dollar mark, but New Castle's distinct island character remains intact. Even the earliest island settlers would recognize the place. Modern hotel visitors following an 1874 New Castle guidebook could find every historic site still in place—and freely accessible. What they probably wouldn't find is a parking space.

TOP: *The seal of New Castle, formerly the provincial capital of colonial New Hampshire. (ATH)*

OPPOSITE TOP: *Pfc. Norman E. Hope serving at Camp Langdon during World War II. Today, the barracks area is the site of the "Commons" picnic area near the small New Castle beach. (NEH)*

OPPOSITE BOTTOM: *Norman Hope at nearby Fort Stark just up the road in New Castle. Hope is standing beside the twelve-inch gun at Pit #1, Battery Hunter. No enemy ever attacked and the crumbling remains of the fort are now part of a state park scarcely half a mile from Wentworth by the Sea. (NEH)*

# THE MIGHTY WENTWORTHS

**W**entworth by the Sea stands at the highest point of Great Island, the perfect location for a summer resort. But location isn't everything. Names count, too.

To draw visitors from great distances and to distinguish themselves from the competition, early hotel owners needed names as big as the buildings themselves. Just across the river in York, Maine, once stood The Passaconnaway, a hotel named for the Indian sagamore who welcomed the first New England colonists in peace and who, legend says, lived a hundred years. Kittery, Maine, boasted the grand Champernowne Hotel, named for an ancestor of Sir Walter Scott who settled here in 1634. The famous Farragut Hotel to the south in Rye offered dramatic views of the ocean and the Isles of Shoals. America's first admiral, David Glasgow Farragut, once a popular guest at Portsmouth Naval Shipyard, loaned his prestigious name to the hotel. Born in Tennessee and a veteran of the War of 1812, Farragut became a northern hero when he sided with the Union as a commander in the Civil War.

In seacoast New Hampshire history, no name carried more clout than Wentworth. To eighteenth-century New Hampshire, the Wentworths were the Kennedys, the Rockefellers, and the Roosevelts, all rolled into a single dynasty. They were rich, political, and powerful. The Wentworths lived in great mansions, several of which still survive. In the last sixty years before American independence, they ruled colonial New Hampshire.

OPPOSITE: *Royal Gov. Benning Wentworth, a Portsmouth native, became the most powerful leader in New Hampshire, second only in influence to King George himself before the Revolution. His fame as the region's wealthiest aristocrat made him the perfect namesake for the grand and luxurious Wentworth Hotel a century later. (ATH)*

They wore the finest clothes, controlled the most land, hosted the best parties, and gave rise to the juiciest scandals in the region.

In short, the Wentworths provided the perfect moniker for a budding hotel. Owners have tinkered with the name for more than a century and a quarter. Some locals mistakenly believe it was first called Wentworth Hall, but no reference to that effect appears in any documents discovered so far. Wentworth Hall refers, instead, to a White Mountains country inn. The 1869 Wentworth still survives in Jackson, New Hampshire and was named for a Civil War general from that region. The reference most likely refers to Benning Wentworth's mansion. The hotel began simply as The Wentworth and sometimes casually Wentworth House. That was later formalized to the Wentworth Hotel and sometimes to Hotel Wentworth, then to Wentworth by the Sea (with and without hyphens) to its current version. Always the original vision survives.

Historian John Albee in his 1884 *New Castle: Historic and Picturesque* takes full credit for picking the Wentworth title. He writes:

> The privilege of naming the Wentworth was granted to the present writer by the original proprietor, and was chosen on account of its proximity to the old Wentworth mansion, and its popular, widely known associations; and also because the name itself is well sounding, and I dare say, slightly aristocratic.

The Wentworths' Tory dynasty faded with the American Revolution, replaced by New Hampshire patriot names like Langdon, Stark, Sullivan, Whipple, Dearborn, Bartlett, and Thornton. But while Yankees were able to cast off the chains of their British king, they remained fascinated with the trappings of "American" royalty. That fact is supported by the large and sometimes confusing array of Wentworth-family buildings that survive to this day. At least five eighteenth-century Portsmouth houses, most of them public museums, are directly associated with the Wentworth name, and the family's wealth created some of the finest architecture in the area.

ABOVE: *Artist's conception of the Native American sagamore Passaconnaway, for whom both a seacoast hotel and a New Hampshire mountain are named. (JDR)*

OPPOSITE TOP: *The Champernowne, in Kittery Point, Maine, visible from the Wentworth, was named for a relative of Sir Walter Scott. (JDR)*

OPPOSITE BOTTOM: *The famous Farragut Hotel in nearby Rye, New Hampshire, was almost as luxurious as the Wentworth. It was named after the esteemed Admiral David Farragut. (ATH)*

TOP: *The early Wentworth "Great House," built around 1695 was torn down in 1926. Portions are on display at the Metropolitan Museum of Art. (ATH)*

BOTTOM: *The 1716 brick MacPhaedris-Warner house still stands in downtown Portsmouth. It was temporarily home to Benning Wentworth, before his move to the mansion at Little Harbor. (JDR)*

The Wentworth family grew from humble farming stock. Elder William Wentworth, from whom all three royal New Hampshire governors were descended, arrived from England in 1638. He farmed land first in Exeter, then in Wells, Maine, and settled finally in rustic Rollinsford, New Hampshire.

Elder William's grandson John Wentworth was a Portsmouth sea captain who worked his way up the political food chain from councilman to court justice. He was appointed lieutenant governor of the entire colony in 1717. His was the original Wentworth mansion, built around 1695, which stood conspicuously in Portsmouth's South End. The beautiful interiors of the Wentworth Great House were well known when the New Castle hotel got its name in 1874, although few locals may have actually glimpsed the ornate interior. Sadly, it was a victim of the Colonial Revival, pulled down in 1926, its fine wood-paneled rooms turned into an exhibit at the Metropolitan Museum of Art in New York City. Other surviving remnants are also on view today at the Winterthur Museum in Delaware.

Although John Wentworth was lieutenant to the governor who presided over both Massachusetts and New Hampshire, his son Benning became far more powerful when New Hampshire got a separate royal governor in 1741. Almost a king in his own colony, Benning also held the lucrative title of surveyor to the King's Woods. The British wanted tall straight timber for ship masts, and New Hampshire had it. Benning made a lucrative business of granting townships as New Hampshire extended west into what is now Vermont. Bennington, in southern Vermont, for example, was named in his honor. Initially Benning lived downtown in Portsmouth, where he rented a brick mansion, now the MacPhaedris-Warner House museum. Benning wanted to make the 1716 building the governor's mansion. When the colonial assembly refused to purchase the stately home from his sister, he built his own mansion on the edge of town at Little Harbor.

Arguably the most interesting house in New Hampshire, Benning Wentworth's mansion was rumored to have had fifty-two rooms. In an eclectic design that still baffles architects, Benning Wentworth started with an old warehouse and

The WENTWORTH

Is in New Castle, County of Rockingham, N.H., an island town containing about one square mile, lying between the Piscataqua River and Little Harbor.

New Castle, though apparently so irregular in form, is in fact very regular, being almost a perfect square with jutting points of land at the four corners, like the bastions of a fort. Its ancient name was Great Island. In 1693, in the reign of King William and Mary, it was incorporated under the name of New Castle for the consideration of three peppercorns to be paid annually. The town is largely in arrears to the British crown for peppercorns, and owes not only these but its legal allegiance, never having received any charter

ABOVE: *Gov. Benning Wentworth's rambling mansion on Little Harbor was the inspiration for the Wentworth Hotel. Its owner offered tours of the house to visitors while the Wentworth was being built. Today as the Wentworth-Coolidge Mansion, it belongs to the state of New Hampshire and the descendants of Benning's imported lilacs still bloom in the yard. (PER)*

LEFT: *Sketches of the mansion appear in early Wentworth brochures. (ATH)*

assembled a series of odd-shaped additions into a rambling mansion. The epitome of elegance, Benning's 1753 home required a full-time master carpenter, who was forever adding sections. Legend holds that the mantlepiece in the so-called council chamber alone took an artist one year to carve. Visitors then as now got the best view of the Wentworth House from the water on Little Harbor. Today the restored building with forty or so rooms is owned by the State of New Hampshire.

Victorians were fascinated by the old governor's home in all its fading majesty even as the Wentworth Hotel was conceived and built. Owner William Pusey Israel was all too happy to provide guided tours to seacoast visitors and even advertised the house in a broadside in the 1870s.

Benning, the popular story goes, got very lonely in his enormous home on the outskirts of the city. He had outlived his wife and all three of their sons. When the richest, most powerful man in New Hampshire proposed to an attractive Portsmouth woman, she declined his offer and married a ship captain. When the captain was suddenly impressed into military service for seven years, locals considered it Benning's revenge. The elderly governor's eye then fell upon Martha Hilton, his twenty-something housekeeper. Portsmouth historian Charles Brewster depicted Martha as "a careless laughing bare-footed girl lugging a pail of water in the street with a dress scarcely sufficient to cover her decently." Criticized for her devil-may-care manner, Martha was said to have responded brazenly: "No matter how I look, I shall ride in my chariot yet."

The facts are somewhat less scandalous. Martha Hilton was a member of a respectable local family. The Hiltons, who had settled in the region in 1623, had even deeper roots than the Wentworths. According to Philip Young's *Revolutionary Ladies,* young Martha was twenty-three when she wed the sixty-three-year-old governor, a man not noted for his charm, good health, or appearance. The May-December marriage rocked the citizenry. Henry Wadsworth Longfellow, in a poem that seems lifted directly out of Brewster's chronicles, set the titillating tale of Martha Wentworth into rhyme. It was published in 1863 in the hugely popular *Tales of a Wayside Inn,* the same collection

ABOVE: *Martha Hilton, who married the royal governor—who was forty years her senior—was depicted in Victorian legend as a barefoot maid with high social aspirations. Henry Wadsworth Longfellow fictionalized her marriage in the popular poem "Lady Wentworth," which appeared in his collection* Tales of a Wayside Inn. *(PPL)*

that includes Longfellow's equally romanticized account of Paul Revere's midnight ride. Illustrated versions of the poem show a portly, aristocratic old man and a pretty, very young scullery maid, sometimes carrying an oaken water bucket.

In the poem, Benning invites the most prestigious social families in the seaport capital to a sixtieth birthday dinner at his mansion—the Langdons, the Lears, the Penhallows, and the highly influential Reverend Arthur Browne, of Queen Anne's Church. The royal governor dramatically reveals his intentions toward his housekeeper, Miss Hilton, and requests to be married on the spot. When the rector responds with stunned silence, according to Brewster, the host shouts, "As the governor of New Hampshire, I command you to marry me."

The birthday party was almost certainly a poetic device. The Langdons and the Lears, for example, are best known for their historic roles in Portsmouth after the Revolution. Colonial revival poetry was long on romance and short on facts. It is likely that only a few close family members were present, historian Young points out. Martha had been compelled to take employment as a servant only after her father was killed in service to the crown at the battle at Louisbourg. Still, she was the maid, and the whole event was an embarrassment to the Wentworths.

Few in the seacoast in the nineteenth century would have been unfamiliar with the work of the famous romantic poet. Longfellow, who frequently traveled from Cambridge to his hometown in Portland, Maine, reportedly stopped by Portsmouth in 1871, just two years before the Wentworth Hotel was built. He toured a number of the town's historic houses, including the old governor's mansion at Little Harbor. When *Tales of a Wayside Inn* was republished, the author added a footnote to his poem, "Lady Wentworth." According to Wentworth family members, he explained, there had not actually been a crowd of local socialites at the event, just the family and the Reverend Browne. Martha Hilton was, by this tale, closer to thirty-five years old and wore not a silk gown, as Longfellow stated, but a calico dress and a white apron.

After the governor's death in 1770, Lady Wentworth married Michael Wentworth from Yorkshire. Technically the

TOP: *This is possibly a portrait of the real Martha Hilton Wentworth Wentworth. (NHHS)*

BOTTOM: *The poet Henry Wadsworth Longfellow was fascinated by tales of the aristocratic Wentworths. When the poem appeared in the Atlantic in 1872, Longfellow, like his character Benning Wentworth, was a well-known, wealthy senior citizen whose wife had died. (JDR)*

title "lady" does not apply at all, as Benning had no noble title, just a political one. Young notes that Michael had been the governor's lawyer during the drafting of his will and would have been privy to the fact that Martha was the sole beneficiary of Benning's enormous fortune. When George Washington toured Portsmouth with his secretary Tobias Lear in 1789, a visit to Michael and Martha Wentworth at Little Harbor was high on his social itinerary. Michael died in 1797 and Martha outlived him, too.

The most lovable of the Wentworth dynasty was another John, son of Benning's brother Mark, a rich merchant. Born in Portsmouth, he attended Harvard, where he was a classmate of future president John Adams. Unlike his regal uncle, John had a working relationship with the people he governed. But revolution was in the air. Sympathetic with colonial protest, John Wentworth once described the Stamp Act as an "odious tax" and wrote to England in protest of the taxes that were creating dissent in New England. He initiated the construction of New Hampshire highways, rebuilt the lighthouse at New Castle and held public forums in a new statehouse in the center of Portsmouth's Parade, now known as the central Market Square.

But Royal Governor John Wentworth was in the wrong place at the wrong time. Soon after the local patriots raided the fort at New Castle, he and his wife, Frances, and their young son were forced to evacuate their rented home on Pleasant Street in Portsmouth. John had not much liked the "little hut," as he once described the small but ornate house (now a nursing home on the shore of the South Mill Pond). More, he hated leaving his summer home, which was at the time under construction in the distant wilderness of Wolfeboro, the first New Hampshire vacation house, which he was never to complete.

There has always been a hint of guilt in Portsmouth for ejecting poor John Wentworth from his hometown. Though he certainly knew the names of the rebel leaders—his neighbors— who had stolen King George's gunpowder and cannon, he never turned them in for what was certainly a hanging offense. After sitting out the American Revolution in Europe, the Wentworths, like a great many other New England Loyalists, resettled in Canada. John was eventually appointed royal governor of Nova Scotia. Visitors to Halifax can still see his magnificent mansion there, still occupied by its latest royal appointee and guarded by volunteer sentries in red coats and Beefeater-style hats.

Besides great architecture, the aristocratic Wentworths left behind great stories. John and Frances, for example, were cousins who had been close as children. When John went off to England, Frances married Theodore Atkinson, a prominent Portsmouth businessman whose family had also been important in New Castle politics. Within a few years the king was seeking to replace John's Uncle Benning, then ill and elderly and becoming a bit of an embarrassment. John Wentworth, who had the common touch, was the natural successor. Soon after John became royal governor in 1769, Theodore Atkinson died. Ten days after her husband's funeral, Frances Atkinson exchanged her mourning dress for a wedding gown and married her rich and handsome cousin John.

This shocking Wentworth tale too was set to rhyme. The year after the Wentworth opened in 1875, *The Galaxy: A Magazine of Entertaining Reading* published an epic 232-line poem about the passions of John and Frances. Also entitled "Lady Wentworth," the poem, by Nora Perry, chronicled a second Wentworth bride who had gotten her man in defiance of social standards.

Years later, rumors of scandal drifted back to Portsmouth from Nova Scotia. Tales of Frances's infidelity to John are central to a bestselling historical novel by Thomas Raddall. A paperback cover of *The Governor's Lady* from 1955 bears the steamy subtitle, "Not even an army could satisfy her needs." Adding insult to injury, at age seventy-five John Wentworth was forced to flee Halifax with Frances to avoid debtor's prison due to unpaid expenses they had accumulated during his royal reign in Nova Scotia.

Amazingly, more grand homes with Wentworth family connections survive from the eighteenth century, each with a fascinating story. The Joshua Wentworth House, for example, stands on the campus of Strawbery Banke Museum, not far from

TOP: *The governor and his lady rented this house on Pleasant Street in Portsmouth and were building a summer home in distant Wolfeboro. Today this is the Mark H. Wentworth Home. (JDR)*

BOTTOM: *John and Frances Wentworth later built a grand mansion in Halifax, Nova Scotia, where he served as lieutenant governor. Government House is occupied today by his successor and guarded by local militia reenactors. (JDR)*

TOP: *The Joshua Wentworth house is today on the campus of Strawbery Banke Museum near the famous Stoodley's Tavern. (JDR)*

MIDDLE: *The Wentworth-Gardener house in Portsmouth's South End is open for tours. It was once owned and restored by the famous photographer and New England writer Wallace Nutting. (FC)*

BOTTOM: *Sarah Wentworth Purcell was a niece of Governor Benning Wentworth. She became a widow and a patriot during the Revolution. Her house is now the home of the Portsmouth Historical Society. (JDR)*

the site of the family's first Great House, which is now at the Metropolitan. Joshua, unlike his Tory relatives, was a militia colonel during the Revolution and went on to serve in both the New Hampshire Senate and the House of Representatives. Threatened by urban renewal in 1973, the two-hundred-year-old building was floated downriver from Portsmouth's North End to the South End by barge.

The jewel of the South End, the 1760 Wentworth-Gardner Mansion is considered among the finest examples of Georgian-style architecture in New England. This was the showplace of Mark Hunking Wentworth, brother of Benning and the father of the unlucky governor John Wentworth. The famous antiquarian Wallace Nutting restored the mansion on the water's edge in the early twentieth century and used it as the backdrop for a series of highly collectible, hand-tinted Colonial Revival photographs. Nutting rebuilt a chain of historic New England homes to attract a freewheeling new wave of motorcar tourists, but World War I cut short his entrepreneurial dream. Today the elegant house, with its symmetrical facade, painted murals, and wood siding, is run by a volunteer nonprofit organization. The Tobias Lear home, visited too by George Washington, is next door.

Another independent house museum, the John Paul Jones House, owned by the Portsmouth Historical Society, was built in 1758 for Sarah Wentworth, niece of Benning, by her husband, Gregory Purcell. When he died, leaving her with debts and eight children, the widow Purcell was forced to rent rooms in her two-and-a-half-story gambrel-roof home. Legend says that the naval hero John Paul Jones twice lodged at the house while waiting for two ships, *Ranger* and *America,* to be completed in the shipyard of none other than John Langdon, the man who led the raid on the New Castle fort.

As evidence that truth is stranger than fiction, a final eighteenth-century Wentworth mansion lies in pieces in boxes at this writing, ready to be reassembled like a giant three-dimensional puzzle. Paul Wentworth built his mansion in Rollinsford, New Hampshire, the town where Elder William Wentworth finally settled in the mid-1600s. Paul's father, Ezekiel, was the son of Elder William, and Ekeziel stayed on the farm while his brother

Samuel sought his fortune in Portsmouth and New Castle and founded the dynasty there.

In 1936 his elegant home was sold by a Wentworth descendant and moved beam and brick to be rebuilt in Dover, Massachusetts. In 2002, when the land under the house was sold, the owner offered it back to the town of Rollinsford. A nonprofit group plans to rebuild the lost Paul Wentworth mansion.

This Paul Wentworth is not to be confused with a later Paul Wentworth from the region who landed on the fence as the family divided itself during the Revolution as either patriot or loyalist. Even as John Paul Jones was making his famous raids on England, this Paul Wentworth was working with Benjamin Franklin in France. It took one hundred years for history to discover what Franklin suspected—that Paul Wentworth had been a double agent spying for the British.

Loved, despised, admired, feared, and envied—it was impossible not to react to the mighty Wentworth clan. Only their name was big enough for the Wentworth Hotel, which would soon grow larger than all the famous Wentworth mansions put together.

ABOVE: *The Paul Wentworth house is currently being restored in Rollinsford, New Hampshire, after having been located for decades in Massachusetts. (RHS)*

# HERE THEY COME

The story of the Wentworth Hotel began to take shape on October 21, 1873, when the schooner *Mary Ann McCann* returned to New Castle loaded with 220,000 feet of lumber from Bangor, Maine. According to the *Portsmouth Chronicle*, it took workmen ten days just to unload the raw material at the western end of the island. The Campbell family, owners of Campbell Cottage, were going to build their dream hotel. Charles Campbell and his wife, Sarah, had been buying up tracts of land on the rise just above their summer home on Goose Island. Their cottage had been a popular guesthouse for summer visitors for two decades. Now with the tourist trade picking up, the Campbells had found an investor, Daniel E. Chase, a relative on Sarah's side of the family, who owned one of the largest distilleries in New England. Chase had come from Somerville, Massachusetts, to help tame the rocky New Hampshire bluff with its stunning ocean view.

The year 1873 was a banner one for tourism. Portsmouth launched the biggest in a series of homecoming weekends. The Return of the Sons and Daughters celebration marked the 250th anniversary of the region's settlement. Stirred by the revival in all things colonial, families who had left old Portsmouth decades earlier during its economic doldrums returned in droves for fireworks, parades, banquets, and other pageantry. Downtown merchants in friendly competition festooned each entrance to the center of the city with huge arches. Arches and buildings were

ABOVE: *A series of homecoming weeks attracted families who had abandoned the port city during poor economic times. This image shows a decorated building during the 1873 Return of the Sons and Daughters, an early tourist event. The building is today a garage on Court Street in Portsmouth. (ATH)*

OPPOSITE: *Tourism began in the seacoast before the Civil War. Colonial Revival visitors stayed at a number of New Castle guesthouses to take the air and walk the rural roads. (ATH)*

ABOVE: *Maren Hontvet survived the 1873 midnight attack by murderer Louis Wagner on Smuttynose Island in the Isles of Shoals. Her story has been wildly fictionalized and widely read in the book* Weight of Water, *by Anita Shreve. (ATH)*

lavishly decorated in patriotic bunting, fresh green boughs, garlands of flowers, and massive carved wooden eagles tinted gold.

This was also the year of the infamous Smuttynose Murders. Earlier that March two immigrant women had been killed on a frigid moonlit night at the Isles of Shoals. The killer, Louis Wagner, rowed a stolen dory from Portsmouth past New Castle and out to Smuttynose Island. Wagner apparently intended to rob his former employer, John Hontvet, a Norwegian fisherman who had been stranded in Portsmouth for the night waiting for a shipment of bait. Wagner had lived on the island for a time with the Hontvets and another couple, and knew the island cottage well. Surprised by a guest sleeping in the kitchen, Wagner strangled her and killed her sister-in-law with an ax, as Hontvet's wife, Maren, escaped out a window.

In that same year, the Oceanic, another grand wooden hotel, opened on Star Island, just across Gosport Harbor from Smuttynose. In her deposition to police, Maren Hontvet reported that the morning after the murders, half frozen and still dressed in her nightclothes, she could hear the hammering of construction crews building the new hotel. She had called to the workmen at nearby Star Island for help, but they had not heard her cries. Coincidentally, the Oceanic and Wentworth by the Sea, visible to each other, are the only two seaside hotels in the region that survive from that era.

The enormous publicity surrounding Wagner's trial brought even more visitors to the area as Wagner insisted on his innocence. According to one report, tourists flocked to Smuttynose Island, cutting blood-spattered souvenirs of wood from the floors and walls of the Hontvet house. The *Portsmouth Chronicle* noted that no previous summer had brought more strangers to the region. Some hotel visitors had been required to sleep under billiard tables and on verandas, while large dining rooms had been full almost to the point of suffocation. Besides the Wentworth and a number of smaller guesthouses, the Ocean House was going up in Rye, the Sagamore at Frost's Point, and the Dow Farm in Wallis Sands. The well-established Curtis House on the other side of New Castle island was later joined by the Sea Breeze.

"But during this coming year," the *Chronicle* reported in

September 1873, "this [room shortage] should be obviated by the completion of a large hotel which is now having the foundation laid in on the banks of Little Harbor."

Although the Wentworth Hotel became and remains the largest structure in New Castle, it was far from the first lodging house there. In fact, as the seat of the first provincial government of New Hampshire, Great Island can boast at least one of the nation's oldest inns and more than 350 years in what is now called the hospitality industry. Historians can track the evolution of public houses because special licenses were required then, as now, to lodge people, to feed them, and to brew and serve alcoholic beverages. In the 1700s alone, provincial records show nearly two dozen men and women licensed to run New Castle taverns and ordinaries.

Earlier still, George Walton, who came to New Castle via Boston and Exeter, was allowed to buy the first known license to operate an inn or ordinary on Great Island in 1649 (some say 1647). Walton was apparently also a tailor, and with a license to brew alcoholic beverages, he was a very early vintner at the Sign of the Anchor. Walton's inn was close enough to the site of the first fort to make it a handy stopping-off point for governing officials. Two centuries later, Sarah Campbell's father, also a tailor, would settle in very nearly the same spot, where they ran a New Castle store.

Walton lost his license a few years later for running a disorderly house. A town legend suggests that a brawl broke out under Walton's roof and the guests destroyed all early records of Great Island for reasons unknown. Town historian Eugene Morrill says the records were actually destroyed by Portsmouth selectmen during early political disputes between the evolving towns. That must certainly make Walton's tavern the site of the nation's first illicit government shredding operation! The provincial records may be gone but, extraordinarily, George Walton's tavern survives as part of a private home overlooking the river just a short walk from the ruins of Fort Constitution, among the oldest surviving structures in the nation.

Early colonial inns often provided spartan accommodations, perhaps just a bed, or part of a bed, in a private house. Others

ABOVE: *If local lore is correct, this building in New Castle must be among the oldest surviving hotels in America. George Walton reportedly ran an "ordinary" for guests here as early as 1647. Architectural historians, however, indicate that no evidence of the original structure has been authenticated. (JDR)*

offered a staff of domestics or slaves and serving maids, private accommodations, and entertainment. As Great Island evolved from a fishing to a shipping center, the range of ordinaries grew. The Atkinson, Jaffrey, and Bell families, among others, were known for their public houses. In hard times, as the thriving economy moved to mainland Portsmouth, a hotel license was a means of earning a living away from the sea. Henry Russell, for example, petitioned the colony for a license in 1682 "to entertain fishermen and Seamen with Diet and Lodging at my house," claiming that he was "Stricken in yeares." A year later, in his request for a tavern license, Joseph Purmont explained that he had a wife and children to feed and that the trading business on Great Island was "very dead."

Samuel Wentworth, initially of Dover and related to Royal Governor Benning Wentworth, operated his seventeenth-century tavern at an early ferry site near where the Portsmouth Yacht Club stands today. His logo, the Sign of the Dolphin, was adopted two centuries later by Wentworth by the Sea, and is still in use in marketing today. The appearance of the dolphin in old hotel brochures has led some history writers to suggest that Samuel Wentworth, rather than Governor Benning Wentworth, was the inspiration for the naming of the hotel. Indeed, an imagined illustration called "Ye Sign of Ye Dolphin" appears in John Albee's 1884 history of New Castle. But early promotional literature for the hotel, much of it apparently written by Albee himself, indicates that the important royal governor Benning, and not his seventeenth-century pub-operating relative, embodied the theme of the new hotel. A painting of Benning Wentworth on a large mirror was installed in the hotel the week it opened. His mansion, too, was often depicted in the earliest hotel literature, while the dolphin motif did not flourish at the hotel until the late 1920s and early 1930s, when it took on an art deco style.

The most famous tavern-related story on Great Island is that of the Stone-Throwing Devil in 1682. Again the hero is George Walton, this time operating a boardinghouse farther west on the island, near the site of the New Castle grammar school today. Walton was then identified as "a Planter." Supernatural business aside, the incident may have risen out of a property dispute. Accusing a neighbor, particularly a female neighbor, of witchery was not uncommon, and it is worth noting that at this time in history the colony of New Hampshire was temporarily under the jurisdiction of the Puritan government of Massachusetts.

Portsmouth journalist and historian Charles Brewster, writing in the mid-1800s, suggested that an elderly woman claimed loudly that George Walton had taken over a piece of land in her field. Legend holds she told witnesses that Walton would never enjoy a quiet time while he lived on his stolen bit of property. Her comment was taken as an evil spell in an era when belief in witchcraft flourished. Women who expressed themselves in public or defied a magistrate could be sentenced to public whipping or dunking in a local pond. In nearby Hampton, then a Puritan town, Eunice "Goody" Cole became the only New Hampshire woman convicted of witchcraft, and spent many of her elderly years in a Boston jail.

On June 16, 1682, showers of stones fell on George Walton's New Castle house. Visitors ran outdoors to find a gate taken off its hinges and were then themselves pelted with stones. Back inside the house, flying stones crashed through windows. Participants gathered up the stones and laid them on the table, where they shot around the room as if tossed by an invisible hand.

This published account comes from preacher Cotton Mather, best known for his deadly role as a judge in the Salem witch trials a few years later. A very detailed report of the devilish phenomenon labeled *Lithobolia* appeared in 1699 in London in a pamphlet by Richard Chamberlain. The author claimed that while he was on duty in New Hampshire for the crown he was an "Ocular witness" to the events that plagued George Walton for three full months. The flying stones, Chamberlain wrote, ranged in size from pebbles to the size of a man's fist. Some were cold, some as hot as if they had come from an oven. One day a spit from the stove fell down the chimney and a clothes iron was found on the lawn. Walton and others were reportedly pelted with stones and heavy objects on other occasions. Visitors heard the sound of strange hoofbeats. Walton's

ABOVE: *A fantastical image of poor Eunice "Goody" Cole illustrated a nineteenth-century collection of poems by John Greenleaf Whittier. (ATH)*

anchor leapt from his boat and into the water. Then suddenly the incidents stopped.

One generation's lore is another generation's lure. Early owners of the Wentworth Hotel were quick to capitalize on the supernatural tale and the story of the Stone-Throwing Devil appeared prominently in early marketing brochures. John Albee, whose town history may have been paid for by Frank Jones, and who may have had a financial interest in the Wentworth land speculation, devoted eight pages to the story in his 1884 town history. Intrigued by the dark side, Albee found a host of religious and political reasons to explain the devilish phenomenon. The split between New Castle and Portsmouth was reaching its peak at this time, Albee noted. Chamberlain, who chronicled the story during his stay at Walton's tavern, was a lawyer representing the Masonian Proprietors, descendants of John Mason who had inherited the colony of New Hampshire. As the proprietors were hoping to extract income from local landowners, he and Walton would have been unpopular.

ABOVE: *The "rock-throwing devil" is a popular occult tale in New Castle history. The story, once interpreted as witchcraft, makes more sense when explained in light of the surrounding religious, political, and social conditions of the time. (JA)*

Archaeologist Emerson 'Tad' Baker has studied the *Lithobolia* phenomenon for years and sees the incident as a precursor to the famous Salem witch trials a decade later. He points out that Walton and his wife, Alice, were also Quakers in an era when Quakers could be punished by death in Puritan Massachusetts. The Congregational church on Great Island was being supplanted by the Anglican church in Portsmouth, leading to even more upheaval. Baker also points out that the Waltons, now elderly, had outlived a number of their own children and were raising their grandchildren, who stood to inherit the Walton wealth. It seems likely that the youngsters, who figure prominently in *Lithobolia*, may have been behind the mysterious stoning, Baker theorizes. George Walton was reportedly hit thirty or forty times, one missile cracking his head, and died three years later.

Tavern licenses were continually issued in New Castle, but except for the activity in its many forts, New Castle slips from the spotlight in the 1700s and early 1800s. Famous Revolution-ary-era visitors like George Washington, the Marquis de Lafayette, and John Paul Jones stayed at inns and private board-inghouses in downtown Portsmouth. Young Louis-Philippe, later to become King Louis XVI of France, vacationed nearby at a home on Sagamore Creek. But New Castle island, isolated by its ferries and later by toll bridges, remained just off the beaten path.

It wasn't until the mid-nineteenth century that getting off the beaten path became a new reason to travel. The growth of crowded noisy cities, thick with residential and factory pollu-tants, made vacations in northern New England desirable. Better roads, trains, and large ships made the trip possible. The rise of the new middle class made vacations affordable.

The history of tourism in New Hampshire inevitably focuses on the White Mountains, tallest of the New England peaks, and away from its minuscule coastline. Hardy vacationers like *Walden Pond* writer Henry David Thoreau, of Massachusetts, were singing the praises of the Granite State as early as the 1840s. The first hotel appeared on the summit of Mount Wash-ington in 1852 and was demolished in 1884. The Tip-Top House was built there in 1853 and survives. Both buildings were protected against "the world's worst weather" by stone walls out-side their wooden walls. Early rusticators led the summer migra-tion from the cities to the stupendous natural wonders—the fast-flowing Flume, the smooth curved Basin, and Profile Lake just below what was until recently the Old Man of the Moun-tain. Classic New Hampshire hotels sprang up as the railroads cut through the Granite State.

It's worth remembering that the first Europeans to explore the White Mountains were coming from the seacoast area. As early as the 1620s, Captain Walter Neale and a small party of British explorers cut their way inland to the clear New Hamp-shire lakes and on to the mountains. This exploration by the Laconia Company, the corporate investors from England, did not turn up the hoped-for gold. Neale, who became the first gov-ernor of the New Hampshire colony at New Castle, collected white crystals of unknown value during his expedition to the White Mountains. He named the snow-capped mountains there

ABOVE: *The former "Old Man of the Mountain" in Franconia Notch, New Hampshire. (RMC)*

OPPOSITE TOP: *The earliest guesthouse on the Isles of Shoals was operated for a time by Thomas and Eliza Laighton. The foundation of the Mid Ocean House of Entertainment is still visible on Smuttynose. (ATH)*

OPPOSITE BOTTOM: *The Sagamore House was short lived. When the Wentworth opened, this large hotel was located directly across Little Harbor at Rye. It burned in 1875 and was never rebuilt. (ATH)*

TOP: *Poet John Greenleaf Whittier of nearby Amesbury, Massachusetts. (JDR)*

BOTTOM: *In his era, poet Whittier gathered tales for his popular ballads by visiting seacoast New Hampshire and tenting on the beach with other tourists. (ATH)*

Crystal Hills. Unfortunately for Neale, the crystals were worthless, and so was the name.

The rise of the tourist trade along the seacoast paralleled its growth in the state's mountains and lakes. Visitors came initially for the view, preferring spots with wide scenic vistas. The Cliff House, perched on a dramatic rock formation in nearby Ogunquit, Maine, opened in 1872, just two summers before the Wentworth. To the south, in Hampton, New Hampshire, where as many as a quarter of a million sun worshippers may now gather on a July or August day, the earliest public house appeared in 1820 atop Great Boar's Head, a rock formation that rises 160 feet above the sea. The hugely popular poet John Greenleaf Whittier, of nearby Amesbury, Massachusetts, found the beach uncrowded when he pitched his tent there in the mid-nineteenth century. The sea was a place to cast off cares and to blend with the past. That is Whittier's message as expressed in this excerpt from his poem "Hampton Beach." This theme of deep relaxation in nature and renewal also rang true with early Wentworth guests. Here is the first stanza:

> Good by to pain and care! I take
> Mine ease to-day :
> Here where these sunny waters break,
> And ripples this keen breeze, I shake
> All burdens from the heart, all weary thoughts away.

By the time of the arrival of the Wentworth, seaside hotels were a common sight. In nearby Rye alone, the Drake, Farragut, Ocean, Atlantic, Washington, Marden, and other lodging houses were already in operation. One of the region's earliest and boldest hotel entrepreneurs, Thomas Laighton, realized the potential for selling the healthy properties of the sea to city visitors. After unsuccessful forays into politics, whaling, and the newspaper trade, Laighton moved his wife and two children from downtown Portsmouth to isolated White Island at the Isles of Shoals, where he became the lighthouse keeper in 1839. That same year he purchased two of the islands, Hog and Smuttynose, without knowing quite what to do with them.

ABOVE: *A one-woman public relations machine, the poet Celia Thaxter, the daughter of Thomas and Eliza Laighton, released* Among the Isles of Shoals *in 1873. Her romantic and dramatic tales of the sea drew visitors in droves to her family hotels on Appledore and Star Islands and are still in print today. (PER)*

OPPOSITE TOP: *The Appledore House was owned and operated by the Laighton family. It burned in 1914. (ATH)*

OPPOSITE BOTTOM: *The original Oceanic, built on Star Island in 1873, burned after only a few seasons. Rebuilt in 1875, the Oceanic, along with the Wentworth, is the only grand hotel on the New Hampshire seacoast. (ATH)*

For a time Laighton tried raising sheep on Hog Island, but that venture flopped as well. He ran a store on Smuttynose and prospered selling liquor to the "heathen" fishermen on Star Island just a few minutes' row across Gosport Harbor. He was intrigued by a small inn on Smuttynose called the Mid-Ocean House, which catered to a trickle of summer visitors who walked the rocky shore and bathed in the sheltered cove. Laighton and his family took over operation of the hotel during summers in the 1840s and attracted a few guests, the writer Richard Henry Dana and the young novelist Nathaniel Hawthorne among them. Hawthorne visited with his close friend from Bowdoin College, Franklin Pierce, who became the only American president to hail from New Hampshire. A travel reporter who stopped at the Mid-Ocean House was taken by the fresh sea air and by the isolated, restful island. He was especially struck by Laighton's beautiful eleven-year-old daughter, Celia, who filled each guest's room with fresh flowers from her own small island garden.

The Mid-Ocean House is gone now, but its rock foundation is still visible in the thick grass just up from the cove, not far from the foundation of the Hontvet murder house. From here, living in the Haley House, which still stands on Smuttynose today, Thomas Laighton finally had the entrepreneurial vision of his life. He built a hotel on Hog Island, which he wisely renamed Appledore. Built in 1847, the Appledore Hotel eventually grew to accommodate up to four hundred guests, who arrived by steam ferry. The hotel, visible from the mainland of three states, attracted a loyal clientele, including many artists drawn to the salon of Laighton's now-famous daughter, the poet and artist Celia Thaxter. The Appledore did so well, in fact, that it inspired John Poore, of Massachusetts, to build his copycat hotel, the Oceanic, on Star Island. Poore opened his hotel in 1873, just as Daniel Chase and the Campbells were buying up land to build the Wentworth in New Castle. Their dream, like that of the Laightons, we can assume, was to expand from one small island guesthouse to become owners of a large thriving hotel. The Campbells' dream came true for three short years, then was dashed like a tiny boat against a rocky shore.

# Hotel Rising

I t began as a family affair. The little-known story behind the original Wentworth Hotel reads like genealogy. It begins early in the nineteenth century with Allen Porter, a tailor working at Fort Constitution in New Castle. In 1803 Porter married Margaret Gibbs Appleton Maloon, and the couple moved into a house near the fort on the west side of Wentworth Road, where they also ran a little store. It was their daughter Sarah who married a local boy, Charles Edward Campbell, and together, with help from relatives, these two built the Wentworth. According to at least one report, the Campbells were a hospitable couple who worked at a number of seacoast hotels, including the Appledore Hotel at the Isles of Shoals. By the mid-1800s they had settled comfortably into running their own summerhouse on Campbell Island right on the border of Rye.

With the exception of Margaret Smith, who co-owned and co-managed the hotel with her husband, Jim, the history of the Wentworth is dominated by men. But it all started with Sarah Campbell's family, the Porters, who first speculated in New Castle land, buying and selling an array of plots among others and among themselves.

Rare photographs recently unearthed by Campbell family descendants show a sophisticated young Sarah Campbell in fashionable dark fur wrap and hat, clearly a woman of means. A picture presumed to be Sarah's husband, Charles, reveals a handsome, wide-eyed gentleman sporting a handlebar mustache.

OPPOSITE: *Unidentified Campbell family members pose outside their guest cottage on Campbell Island, with the Wentworth Hotel visible in the distance. The hotel tower and bathhouse indicate that the photograph was taken after the family had lost the hotel to bankruptcy. (CAM)*

We also have a number of previously unpublished pictures of their boardinghouse, the older sister, so to speak, of the Wentworth itself. In one, family members pose on the side lawn near a large covered well, the Wentworth Hotel looming behind them like a distant mountain range. Another shows the original Campbell Cottage with what appears to be Campbell family members and guests posing stiffly at intervals along the building's wraparound porch. A large dog and a small boy stare obediently toward the camera while "the help" cluster at the rear entrance, one man strumming a banjo. That cottage burned just after Christmas in 1901. According to a news report, the Campbells heard the fire upstairs during supper and were able to rescue two children sleeping on an upper floor. The lost house and contents were valued at $9,700, but the family had only $2,500 worth of insurance.

But the Campbells persevered and rebuilt their guesthouses. An early-twentieth-century image shows a three-story structure. One image shows five young children in the front yard.

We don't know when Sarah and Charles first decided to build a hotel on the rocky bluff just above their guesthouse on Campbell Island. Perhaps they saw a letter to the editor of the *Morning Chronicle* soon after the Civil War in May 1866. Signed only with the letter *B*, it reads prophetically: "I wonder that the people of Great Island do not move in the matter of having a good summer hotel, when the place has so many advantages over the others in the neighborhood…The wonder is that the people of the place can sit still and see large and flourishing hotels around them, and not move…in a way to reap the benefits…"

The writer suggested that the townspeople cooperatively purchase stock in a hotel project, or at least that the stockholders of the New Castle toll bridge should. He or she listed eleven reasons why New Castle was the ideal site, including scenery, dramatic views of harbor shipping, convenient nearby shopping for women, access to trains and coaches, dock access for steamers, the lack of flies and mosquitoes, and the most healthy air in the world.

Records indicate that the heart of the hotel site, roughly ten to fifteen acres, was first owned by Alex Batchelder in 1631 and

ABOVE: *Sarah Porter Campbell in her only formal portrait. It was Sarah's family who owned prime New Castle real estate. She invested in the original Wentworth and was related to the financier Daniel Chase. (CAM)*

was probably developed into an orchard. The Trefethens and later the Frosts, both well-known local families to this day, owned the property next. Allen Porter Jr., Sarah's brother, and her sister, Margaret, bought the land from the Frost family. As early as 1858, Allen granted his brother-in-law Charles the right to walk through the property with his livestock in exchange for half the costs of building a gate. Later, Allen and Margaret sold the land to another brother, John Porter, then living in Vermont, who in turn sold it back to his sister Sarah, who sold it to investor Daniel Chase for four thousand dollars.

The Campbells had the land, the dream, the skills and the drive to expand their little business, but not the means. Daniel Chase did. Chase was a successful liquor distiller from Somerville, Massachusetts, and, according to Campbell family oral history, he and relatives boarded at Campbell Cottage during the seacoast tourist boom. Born in the little town of Warner, New Hampshire, Chase worked for a Boston rum distiller, partnered with him and later founded his own profitable distillery. Married fifty years, and the father of five children, Chase was heavily involved in fraternal groups—Knights Templar, Eastern Star, Red Men, Odd Fellows—and rose to the rank of high priest of his Masonic order. A friend described Chase in a speech as a strong honest manly man. The speaker said:

> He embodies the spirit of the old time gentleman in the old Puritan character, touched by the broadening and sweetening of our own later day… In business his name was a symbol of integrity. His heart was big and his hand always open for the good of the city that he loved, for the relief of the unfortunate and for all charities.

Chase was also related to the Campbells on the Porter family side. A surviving leather-bound copy of the Campbell Cottage guest book shows at least two visitors named Chase, though none named Daniel. It is fair to speculate that Charles Campbell proposed his idea for a grand hotel to Chase on a perfect summer afternoon and that the two brother Masons hiked to the top of the bluff to catch a spectacular sunset from the preeminent point in New Castle. Perhaps they climbed a tree to

ABOVE: *Although the photo bears no identification, Campbell family descendants believe this to be a portrait of Charles E. Campbell. After losing the hotel to bankruptcy, Charles stayed on as winter caretaker, then passed the job on to his son. (CAM)*

glimpse the now famous view from the Wentworth windows. If they didn't build a hotel there, someone else would.

One critical gap remained. To raise the biggest hotel on the island, Campbell and Chase needed a good bridge. Visitors to the Oceanic and the Appledore Hotels might accept the long, obligatory steamship ride out to the Isles of Shoals, but not mainland guests. The success of the modern Wentworth resort required service that was fast, affordable, and flawless.

The bridge problem had plagued New Castle for 250 years. Colonial records show petition after petition from citizens begging the government for a solid structure connecting Great Island with what is now Rye. Although bridging the great distance at the Portsmouth end was a daunting task, the shallow point of the Little Harbor inlet was promising. The favored spot was at Blunt's Point not far in from the modern hotel. But a bridge built there in the 1680s was quickly washed away in a storm. According to historian Ray Brighton, petitioners in 1712 complained that they had only two chances each day to wade across at low tide or swim their horses—inconvenient activities in any season, but rendered bone chilling and dangerous in winter. Even when the bridge was approved in 1712, New Castle citizens were too poor to raise sufficient funds by public subscription. According to a 1719 petition from New Castle residents, a few wealthy citizens had covered the cost of building the bridge in 1712. The timber was delivered, but vandals cut loose the raft carrying the lumber and it swiftly disappeared out to sea.

As business migrated off the island, the once booming New Castle economy suffered. But the most compelling arguments for the bridge were military. "The Castle" was effectively the only coastal fort in the state. In a frontal attack, troops could neither retreat nor be reinforced quickly from the mainland. Smugglers, one colonial petition noted, were sneaking in and out of Portsmouth via Little Harbor, evading the tariffs due to the king and later to the State of New Hampshire. Bridges were authorized in the 1700s, and each fell into disrepair. One, reportedly, was destroyed by General John Sullivan to foil British attempts to retake the fort during the Revolution. New Castle citizens were not much happier in 1820, when private investors finally

OPPOSITE TOP: *For at least two decades before the Wentworth was built, Campbell Cottage offered summer accommodations to guests. Family members believe this is the building that burned in 1901. (CAM)*

OPPOSITE BOTTOM: *The guesthouse on Campbell Island, reportedly rebuilt after a fire in 1900. It was recently torn down and replaced by condos. (CAM)*

built three toll bridges at the Portsmouth side of town—from Portsmouth to Shapleigh Island, from Shapleigh to Goat Island, and from Goat to New Castle. Pedestrians paid three cents to cross, equestrians six cents, and carriages $12^{1}/_{2}$ cents. Locals complained that the rates were highway robbery and that the fees stifled the advance of the burgeoning tourist trade.

By the time Charles Campbell, with the help of historian John Albee, began buying up choice cottage lots on the scenic island in 1873 for an as-yet-unknown Massachusetts speculator, plans for a new bridge at that end of town were in the wind. By the time the Wentworth opened in June 1874, bids were being taken to construct a five-thousand-dollar highway bridge through the Davis Farm connecting New Castle and Rye, arriving within a few hundred yards of the grand new hotel. But plans stalled even as the cost of the bridge rose, and for the first season the inlet to Little Harbor just below the hotel remained impassable except by boat. Wentworth Hotel visitors still arrived and departed over Portsmouth toll bridges. The new Wentworth Road bridge was passable by December, and opened just before the hotel's second year in 1875.

The first season of The Wentworth approached with what modern business owners call a soft opening. The local press, not yet under the public relations spell of upcoming owner Frank Jones, whispered a few advance reports.

"Land is changing hands at this seaside resort," the *Portsmouth Journal* reported in March of 1874, "and ere long the town will be renowned for its summer residences."

The new hotel would be "elegantly furnished," the brief notice continued. It was also notable for its modern appliances—in particular, gas would be made right on the premises using what was known as the Tiffany technique. The gas itself was nearly as dangerous as the threat of fire. Just that week an inexperienced eighteen-year-old guest at the Kearsage Hotel in Portsmouth had blown out the light in his room before retiring. A porter on night rounds found the rural boy overcome by gaseous emanations and revived him in the nick of time. A test of the Wentworth gas process by a Springfield, Massachusetts, company proved successful. Meanwhile, a massive mirror

OPPOSITE: *This rare illustration shows the original boxy Wentworth with its roof observation tower. The brochure was released after tycoon Frank Jones had taken ownership, but before the familiar towers and mansard roof were added. (ATH)*

"THE WENTWORTH"

NEW CASTLE, N.H.
· F·W·HILTON & CO · · PROPRIETORS ·

THE WENTWORTH COACH

ROCKINGHAM HOUSE PORTSMOUTH, N.H.

*Real Estate.*

## THE WENTWORTH,

AT NEWCASTLE, 4 MILES FROM PORTSMOUTH, N. H., entirely new, with all modern improvements; location the finest on the coast, commanding the views of Pawtuckaway, Saddleback, Agamenticus and White Mountains, Isles of Shoals, Rye and Hampton Beaches; excellent riding, fishing, boating and bathing facilities; inland, river and ocean being immediately adjacent; pine grove directly behind the house; land-locked harbor of 20 acres for ladies' and children's bathing. Take cars on the Eastern Railroad for Portsmouth, where coaches will be in waiting.

jun13    CHAS. E. CAMPBELL, Proprietor.

surmounted by a portrait of Governor Wentworth was ordered for the grand parlor. The grounds would be improved, but without removing the delightful rustic character of the site.

Chase and Campbell were riding a real estate wave and Chase continued to buy land. That summer the *Portsmouth Journal* reported:

"All the land in Newcastle having a water frontage from Fort Constitution round to the westerly corner of the island on Little Harbor side, has (with the exception of two or three small plots) changed hands within the last eight months; the last remaining piece, the farm of Mr. Chas. E. Simpson, having recently been bought by Rev. J. Albee for Boston parties. The men now employed on the new hotel are engaged for the rest of the season to build cottages, which are to be neat and picturesque, and not expensive."

The Boston party was, of course, Chase, whose original vision for a central hotel complex surrounded by smaller rental cottages anticipated the layout of Wentworth by the Sea to the present day. A person writing to the local paper suggested the area be named Riverdale, but the owners were inclined toward Wentworth Village.

ABOVE: *An early advertisement for the Wentworth in the Portsmouth newspaper. (RMC)*

OPPOSITE TOP: *An early stereoscopic view card shows the Wentworth House soon after its opening in 1874. This structure survives inside the Wentworth by the Sea, renovated and reopened in 2003. (MT)*

OPPOSITE BOTTOM: *Detail of the Wentworth surrounded by trees. This image, the only one known, was uncovered among Campbell family papers. (CAM)*

Newcastle, N. H.

Wentworth House.

Very few photographs of the three-story shoebox design have surfaced. One image shows little more than the flat top of the hotel protruding from a tall stand of pines. An observation room and a large American flag are all that adorn the gravel-covered third floor. Without its famous towers and Mansard roof, the original Wentworth looks crude and unfinished, less appealing even than its plain-Jane cousin the Oceanic on the Isles of Shoals. Early brochure drawings avoid the squat frontal view and favor the more sweeping perspective up the rocky entrance to landlocked Little Harbor from the Rye side of the new bridge, the spot where hotel owners James and Margaret Barker Smith later made their home. The shoebox was wrapped in a spartan wooden porch and topped with an observation tower.

Campbell family records list Charles not only as the original Wentworth owner and manager, but also as the builder. Perhaps, but architectural historian Richard Candee has identified Erastus Mansfield as the hotel's first architect. The budget, according to a local paper, was $50,000 for the building and furnishings, half of what Frank Jones would later spend on his first set of improvements to the hotel a few years later. Mansfield was in the family too, a relative of Daniel Chase. He was listed in the Somerville, Massachusetts city directory simply as "carpenter, real estate." Later, after Chase had abandoned his hotel project in New Hampshire, Mansfield joined on as a liquor distributor for Chase & Company.

By January the Wentworth was framed up to the second story. By March the hotel "upon an eminence" had taken shape and by May residents had grown accustomed to the new silhouette clearly visible from South Street in Portsmouth. Judging from one snippet in the local paper on June 13, the week before the opening of the Wentworth drew hordes of curious visitors. More than six hundred people walked the grounds that Sunday. They had come to see the custom-made furnishings set in place and the new carpets put down.

The first season, largely from word of mouth, was a sellout. All eighty-two "apartments" apparently were assigned. In the final week before opening twenty applications for permanent summer residence arrived by mail and eight more parties subscribed in person. Opening week, the hotel was profusely decorated in streamers of flags and pennants from all nationalities. Popular and classical tunes echoed through the grand parlor from the new eight-hundred-dollar piano delivered from Boston. A new stagecoach, driven by Mr. A. H. White, stood ready to deliver visitors from the house to the city. There was talk of building a new horse railroad along the same route, though it never came to pass.

The panoramic view from the original hotel, not the view of it, mattered most to Mansfield, Chase, and Campbell. The first paid ad in the *Portsmouth Chronicle* in June 1874 immediately claimed it to be the finest location on the coast. Visitors could survey not only the Isles of Shoals, Hampton Beach, and Rye, the ad promised, but also inland to Pawtuckaway, Saddleback, and the White Mountains. An early report in the same newspaper a few days later waxed rhapsodic about the view that also took in Maine and Massachusetts, the river, Little Harbor and the city of Portsmouth just four miles away. "The scene at sunrise and sunset," the writer added, "is as wonderful as fairy land."

Forty visiting Masons from the Boston area saw more than fairyland as the first season closed. According to a piece in the *Portsmouth Chronicle,* the ceremonies began with a hundred-gun salute. Then, with a mystical ceremony orchestrated by their host, the honorary Brother Chase, the fraternal order began a profoundly moving weekend. Chase demonstrated for the group how to line up two lighthouses and triangulate the Shoals from the roof observatory, then pointed out the four eras of the formation of the earth in the stratified rock along Sagamore Creek. The men recited poetry, including "where the sculpins rise," and ate baked flounder precisely at sunrise. As the sun set, "flushed with the glories of the departing day," the group assembled on the rocky shore to envision the Four Eras of the Earth. Singing and praying, the Masonic observers of the Heavens, Earth, Wind, and Sea turned their inspired faces to the west and pronounced the Apothegm.

The rituals of these Masons may seem like odd hotel behavior, but times change. Today's independent cell phone-toting, credit card-waving, SUV-driving travelers live in a radically

ABOVE: *View of Little Harbor from the top of the Wentworth Hotel. The scenery is practically identical today. (ATH)*

different America. Less than a decade after the bloodiest war in the country's history, the first Wentworth visitors lived in a society of strict behavioral codes. Although not as rigid as the class structure in England, American "Victorians" knew the rules as defined by their education, ancestry, age, sex, race, income level, and job status. In nearby Portsmouth, for example, diverse social-religious clubs met simultaneously, but separately. Local chapters of the Knights of Pythias, the Colored Knights of Pythias, and the local Ku Klux Klan kept private clubs on the same street, practically in the same building. While the patriarchy reigned supreme, women-only social groups were also on the rise. Yet on Water Street in Portsmouth, the city's red light district flourished, largely unhampered by local police until the Portsmouth Naval Shipyard forced its closure in 1912.

The mixing of the classes had begun, but the dissolution of social barriers was still almost a century away. Trains and travel, the telegraph, and print publications would see to that. But for the moment, Americans remained highly social beings. Travelers shared trains and carriages, ate in communal dining rooms, used group bathrooms, attended lectures and formal functions together. An African-American family in the 1870s, however, would never have considered a vacation at a popular New England seaside resort. Segregation was implied. The stratification of society ran as deep into the foundation of many early resorts as the layers of rock in the ledges off Sagamore Creek. Bridging the equality gap was still decades away and that gap remained longer in some resort hotels than in the surrounding communities. While people of all races and creeds staffed the hotel and kept the wheels running, the first known black patrons to sign the register at the Wentworth did so long after World War II.

The initial four-page flyer pitched the Wentworth's climatic advantages based on twelve years of U.S. government statistics. New Castle experienced, on average, twenty-eight fewer rainy days than Portland and Boston. There were fewer days of "harsh disagreeable" and "unfertile" easterly winds at New Castle, and the area was slightly cooler in summer. Within weeks of opening, according to the newspaper, the Wentworth was booked solid. Transient visitors paid three dollars per day, while seasonal guests paid from fourteen to twenty-eight dollars per week.

The primary activity at early hotels was simply relaxing. Guests sat on the piazza in rocking chairs and watched the sailing ships gliding between harbor and sea. They lounged on the rocks and read, played cards, and chatted. Eating was the second favorite activity. Physical fitness had not yet come into fashion, but for the vigorous souls the Wentworth offered swimming in the protected bay, horseback riding, sailing, and walking. Carriages and ferries were available for those who wanted to see the sights, go to church, visit the village at New Castle, or shop in the city of Portsmouth.

In August, the second month of the first season, while Sarah Campbell busied herself in the kitchen, a group of boys working at the hotel drew Charles out on the piazza to look at the moon. They returned to a surprise ceremony in which the staff and guests presented the Campbells with an engraved seven-piece silver-plated teaset—a collection still owned by Campbell descendants. Following speeches and toasts, Sarah and Charles led the group in a dance that lasted until the wee hours of the morning.

From the outset, the Wentworth tended toward grandeur. It was going to be a classy place. On Appledore Island, playland of the Boston literati, a guest might attend a masquerade ball at the hotel dressed in discarded lobster shells. At the Wentworth, formality reigned. One written report mentions a large party in 1875 when 250 New Castle residents and summer visitors gathered for the first time. The hotel was filled with flowers, topped by a huge wreath, and decked in banners and flags. The group selected a president and then a vice president from each New England state. Following six toasts, the group heard five speeches. The guests presented their hosts, Mr. and Mrs. Campbell, with a needlepoint picture that read GOD BLESS OUR HOME. Then they all sang the "Reunion Ode" to the tune of "Auld Lang Syne." It was, according to one witness, "the largest and most enjoyable gathering ever known at Great Island."

Every great project needs both a dreamer and an investor. What the Campbells dreamed, Daniel Chase built. Chase was in love with the idea of owning the Wentworth, according to

ABOVE: *One piece of the silver tea set given to Sarah and Charles Campbell during the opening summer of the Wentworth is still in the possession of Campbell descendants in Portsmouth. This engraved plated silver had never been publicly displayed. (CAM/PER)*

New Castle historian John Albee, "but he forgot to count cost." Chase told the newspaper that his first year was a financial success and immediately announced the construction of a new wing for the 1875 season. A year later the papers reported that even more additional apartments, already booked in the busy hotel, were still under construction as late as August. The large wing was "almost a house of itself," the paper reported.

New professional pastry chefs now were on duty, new servants' quarters were built, the billiard room was improved, the stables were enlarged, a "floating stage" was added at the pier, and possibly a new bowling alley was built. That same year, with the approaching centennial of the American Revolution, the Wentworth became Hotel Wentworth. According to the press, "some of the best known people in the country" were staying there, and the season ended on a joyous note.

In the summer of 1876, not only was the new bridge working, but also Wentworth guests could select from two coaches running between New Castle and the train station in Portsmouth. The stage line, run by E. W. Cochrane, was advertised as having the best horses and carriages around. Cochrane also ran the Rockingham House Stable downtown. It would not be long before the Rockingham and the Wentworth Hotels were linked by much more than taxi service. Soon they would be connected by one of Portsmouth's first telephone lines and owned by one of the city's richest men.

The Campbells' joyous reign was rapidly fading. Proprietor Charles Campbell "is doing all he can in his power to add to the comfort of his guests," the newspaper had reported apologetically in the hotel's honeymoon year. Following the second summer Campbell was injured, but not seriously, when he was kicked by a horse. Although they were well-loved New Castle residents, Charles and Sarah now faced daily financial and logistical problems unimagined at their little Campbell Cottage just down the hill. Running a big, posh hotel required a new set of skills and a great deal of stamina.

Local newspaper reports allude to a range of troubles for the startup hotel. A number of visitors fell off the rocks above the bathing area and suffered injuries, and this required the

ABOVE: *Another stereo card view shows what appears to be twin girls on the veranda. The white flag at the top may have read "The Wentworth." (ATH)*

OPPOSITE: *Currently the only known image of the Wentworth interior during Campbell and Chase's brief ownership. The figure standing to the right appears to match the portrait of Charles E. Campbell. The unadorned interior was elaborately decorated by its next owner. (ATH)*

construction of a large wooden stairway down to the water. In 1875 a young man was accidentally shot in the chest at the hotel. The paper offered no further explanation, except to say that Herman Carpenter was "very low, although his physician has hopes of his recovery, if mortification does not ensue." The following summer cottages belonging to Daniel E. Chase were burgled and a whaleboat belonging to the hotel was stolen. A year later Campbell was forced to call in the New Castle constable to oust street toughs from the billiard room after a member of the local Marine Band was mugged on the rural road, apparently by local boys.

An early indication of trouble at the Wentworth was its shifting management. From the outset owner Daniel Chase had come to depend on the assistance of his son Charles Henry Chase. Job Jenness, who also ran the Ocean Bluff Hotel in Kennebunkport, Maine, became comanager in 1876. Both men were apparently replaced at the start of the 1877 season by Mr. Gideon Haynes, who, the newspapers assured patrons, had the required hotel experience to guarantee their satisfaction. The newspapers neglected to mention that Mr. Haynes' experience included a stint as warden at Charlestown Prison in Boston.

Campbell apparently called for help too, enlisting his brother-in-law Dr. Amory Jewett, one of the original investors

in the hotel. When the *Portsmouth Guide Book* first appeared in 1876—the anonymous work of artist Sarah Haven Foster—the pocket-sized volume included a full-page advertisement for the Wentworth. Campbell and Jewett were listed as managers. Jewett had married Sarah Campbell's sister Abigail, and when she died, he married another sister, Margaret Madalenah Porter. A hardworking physician from Massachusetts, Jewett became known as "the smallpox doctor" after contracting the disease from patients. His medical career failing, Jewett apparently joined Campbell as comanager just as the hotel, too, was failing.

There was a national recession in progress. Despite the flood of hotel patrons, the year 1876 was a bad one for American business and for Daniel Chase. He had extended himself too deeply into investments outside the distillery business, which it now appeared he might also lose. The Wentworth, meanwhile, still needed a constant infusion of money to develop. Blood may be thicker than liquor, but despite family connections and his reputation for unswerving integrity, Chase bailed out. This notice appeared in the *Portsmouth Chronicle* of June 11, 1877:

> Daniel E. Chase, distiller, of Boston, has recently failed, and the firm of Thomas E. Call & Sons, of this city find themselves among the list of unsecured creditors to the amount of $1,200.

> Call & Sons was just the tip of the iceberg. In the bankruptcy report issued three days earlier, Daniel Chase left hanging no fewer than ninety-five creditors with unpaid bills ranging from $5.19 to $73,000. Builder Erastus Mansfield stood to lose $2,200. Chase defaulted on payment of $4,700 to Sarah Campbell of New Castle, roughly the price owed for the purchase of the land beneath the Wentworth—not to mention the broken dreams of the Campbell family. Dr. Amory Jewett, who had invested funds inherited from his grandmother in his mother's name, lost $3,500. In all, the Massachusetts District Court reported a warrant on the estate of Daniel E. Chase for an unpaid balance of $369, 376.90.

ABOVE: *Amory Jewett, "the smallpox doctor," married two of Sarah Campbell's sisters. He briefly assisted his brother-in-law Charles in managing the hotel. (WJ)*

But Chase survived. After jettisoning the accumulated debts of the Wentworth and other outside investments, his rum

distillery rebounded and thrived. Chase died thirty years later in 1908 of Bright's disease at the age of seventy-eight, while at his summerhome in West Andover, New Hampshire. His lengthy obituary in the Somerville newspaper listed his every accomplishment, named every dignitary attending the funeral, and even described every floral arrangement—but made no mention of the Wentworth fiasco. Yet Chase and the Campbells had successfully conceived, named, built, and launched their dream hotel on New Castle. Despite a rocky kickoff, under their brief ownership the Hotel Wentworth had become, according to at least one printed report, the biggest hotel north of Boston. Actually the Wentworth was far from the biggest hotel, but its reputation was sizable just the same.

Chase was, in a somewhat eerie way, the prototype of the man who succeeded him, just as his shoebox hotel was the rough draft for the luxurious improvements that followed. The next Wentworth owner was also a self-made man who came to the city from a tiny New Hampshire town. The next man too had big plans. While Chase distilled rum and Frank Jones brewed ale, both men climbed from the bottom to the top of their industry. Each took over a business from an elderly boss and renamed the company for himself. Both died of the same disease. Both men were politically active and driven to succeed in the exploding new American economy.

Frank Jones simply wanted it more. In fact, Frank Jones wanted everything more. He was smarter, tougher, greedier, smoother, richer, cannier, and more ruthless than his predecessor. Where Chase saw a grand hotel on a hill, Jones saw the grandest world-class luxury hotel in New England—and he had the resources to make it happen. He didn't have to ask the bank for help. He owned the bank.

ABOVE: *Another view of visitors clustered on the veranda, this time with a pony cart in the foreground. (ATH)*

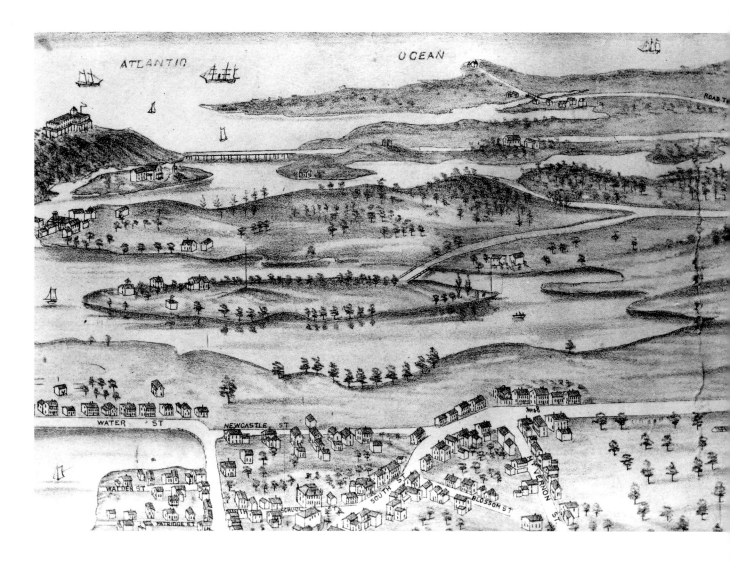

ABOVE: *A corner detail of a much larger 1877 map of Portsmouth includes a sketch of New Castle. The Wentworth is depicted in its original design before Jones's arrival. Campbell Cottage is also visible below the hotel. The Sagamore House in Rye is missing because it burned in 1875. (ATH)*

# Enter the Tycoon

In late-nineteenth-century Portsmouth, Frank Jones was the 10,000-pound gorilla. None since the royal Wentworth family had accumulated the level of his wealth and his clout in seacoast New Hampshire, and so it was fitting, if not inevitable, that Jones would come to own the largest hotel in the region. He would also come to own banks, insurance companies, breweries, racing stables, the world's largest shoe-button factory, real estate, and railroads.

Jones, however, does not burst into the history of the Hotel Wentworth. On April 2, 1879, when the paperwork was filed in the Rockingham County Courthouse, Jones's name did not even appear. The mortgage on the property quietly passed from Francis Hall, a Boston businessman and one of David Chase's key creditors, who had assumed the hotel deed back in 1875, to Frank Hilton & Co. Jones, unlike his predecessor, knew how to find the best help. The Portsmouth newspapers immediately issued the same gushing endorsement of Hilton's managerial skills as they had for the previous Wentworth proprietors, except this time they were right.

Frank W. Hilton was the consummate hotel manager. He knew how to make his employees work and how to make his customers happy. Most important, he knew how to turn his investors' money into more money. Hilton had learned the trade from his father, who ran the DeWitt Hotel in Lewiston, Maine. Taken ill at the Battle of Chantilly, during the Civil War, Hilton

OPPOSITE: *Frank Jones (1832–1902) started as a poor Barrington farm boy and became Portsmouth's wealthiest businessman. Over two decades his wealth and influence transformed the Wentworth into one of the best-known luxury resorts on the Atlantic Coast. (ATH)*

ABOVE: *During the Jones era, the hotel adapted its familiar towers and sloping roof design, which survive to this day. (ATH)*

left the military service, recuperated for eight months, then returned to duty and was wounded at Spotsylvania. After the war, Hilton managed hotels in Chicago and traveled widely with the Pullman Company before returning East. He reportedly managed the Oceanic Hotel at the Isles of Shoals soon after its opening season before finding a permanent position at the Rockingham.

Frank Jones was no stranger to the hotel business either. He eventually owned key hotels in Maine and Boston, but began in 1867 by successfully rehabilitating the old City Hotel in downtown Portsmouth, renaming it the National. Jones even had a ruling hand in the Oceanic at the Isles of Shoals for a short while. His name appears as one of the grantees of the Oceanic in 1879 just as he was buying the Wentworth through Hilton. As brewer of Frank Jones Ale, he also provided hundreds of dining and lodging establishments with their lifeblood.

Born on a farm in Barrington, New Hampshire in 1832, Jones often recalled his first visit to the big city at age sixteen when he drove an oxcart full of charcoal the twenty miles east to Portsmouth. Legend has it that Jones sold that load of charcoal to the manager of the Rockingham Hotel and got his first taste of a gourmet breakfast in the back kitchen. Years later, after buying and renovating the run-down City Hotel a few blocks away, Jones purchased the stately brick Rockingham. In 1875 Jones leased the Rockingham Hotel for five years to his young manager, Frank Hilton, and went off to serve in the U.S. House of Representatives. Under Hilton's management, the Rockingham quickly gained a reputation as one of the finest establishments outside Boston. Jones, it is safe to assume, simply wanted Hilton to do for the Wentworth what he had done for the Rockingham.

Although the paperwork is gone, like almost all the financial records of Frank Jones's empire, we can follow the money trail through the increasing media coverage of the expanding Wentworth Hotel. The *Portsmouth Chronicle* in particular all but tripped over its own tongue in lavish coverage of the renovations under Jones. While hotel founder Daniel Chase had been just another out-of-towner, Jones was Portsmouth incarnate. His

ABOVE: *Before the popular Tally-ho carriage, this early newspaper illustration shows the "four-in-hand" coach transporting visitors the three miles from New Castle to the Portsmouth train station. (LK)*

influence was palpable from the sprawling brick brewery in the city's west end, to the downtown office buildings in Market Square, to the new train steaming into the Eastern Railroad station. The stench and the smoke and the sound of Jones's work were ubiquitous, and had been in Portsmouth by this time for two decades.

Just thirty-two years old in 1864, the young entrepreneur had taken over his brother Hiram's stove shop on Portsmouth's Market Street near the gritty waterfront. After serving a three-year apprenticeship with his older brother, Frank had gone into partnership with Hiram, and in what was the first of many business acquisitions to come had suddenly dissolved the partnership and emerged as sole owner a year later. Hiram, owed six thousand dollars by his little brother, gave up city life to run his own farm in Rye, while Frank accelerated his business interests in Portsmouth. Oddly, his main competition at the time was his other brother, Nathan Jones, who ran the stove shop across the street. Years later, Frank Jones would own most of the brick buildings on the entire row.

Despite all pretense of objectivity, according to Frank Jones's biographer, Ray Brighton, media attention in the nineteenth century, as now, could be measured in a direct ratio of news ink to advertising dollars. Jones learned this fact early. In 1854 Frank Jones purchased the first of many ads in the *Chronicle*. On April 22, 1856, the *Chronicle* returned the favor by plugging young Mr. Jones in an article about his lucrative side business of collecting and selling old rags, which he stockpiled in warehouses. Always alert to a moneymaking opportunity, Jones was able to export a shipload of the discarded rags—about three months' worth of collected inventory—for four thousand dollars. Jones also collected scrap metal for resale and made the papers again, this time as legitimate news, when forty tons of it crashed through the floor of his Portsmouth warehouse.

As the nation was coming apart over issues of slavery and states rights, Jones was getting his act together as a businessman. He bought cheap, added value, and reaped the profits. Not so his brother Hiram, who in 1859, while visiting his mother in Barrington, walked out back into the family privy and quietly slit

ABOVE: *The elegant Rockingham Hotel in downtown Portsmouth was Frank Jones's home base for business. Managed by Frank Hilton, the Rockingham hosted many prestigious visitors and accommodated overflow guests from the Wentworth during peak seasons. Today the building houses condominiums and a restaurant. The popular Rockingham lions still guard the entrances. (ATH)*

his own throat. Two years later Frank Jones married Martha Jones, his dead brother's widow, and adopted her daughter, Emma. The following year, when barefoot farm boys—as he had once been—marched off to die in the Civil War, Frank Jones bought his first brewery and settled in for a steep ride to the top.

Twenty years later, anointed in his own cash flow, Jones was among the new ruling class of corporate Americans. These robber barons, the royal rich spawned by the Industrial Revolution, brokered power and influence and followed their own rules and morality like feudal lords. By age thirty-five, Jones was the youngest mayor in the history of Portsmouth. He then served two terms for New Hampshire in the U.S. House of Representatives, where, despite a tepid career, he helped keep the Navy Yard alive during the military doldrums that inevitably followed the Civil War. But Jones tired of Congress, where he was not master of the game, and his wife grew weary of his high-powered nightlife and his affair with a young socialite. Jones left Washington, D.C., in 1879, the same year he and Hilton acquired the Wentworth Hotel. Like the cartoon character in the Monopoly game, with top hat, tails, and gold-tipped cane, Jones strode home to his Portsmouth empire, which came to include his mansion, his racing stable, his hotels, his railroad, electric power and telephone utilities, and a winning hand of real estate and business holdings. He also came home with some important Washington contacts: Three of his congressional colleagues would become president of the United States, and they would not forget the lavish Mr. Jones.

Now an "elder" statesman, though still in his early forties, Jones was momentarily distracted from his role as overlord of the seacoast by one last political campaign. He decreed that he would become governor. But Jones had made as many enemies in New Hampshire politics as he had cronies. Although he campaigned again as a common man, a former farm boy from the boondocks, opponents pointed out that his vast wealth had not benefited the general public at all, other than to get them drunk. The idea of an ale-making governor in an era of evolving temperance had an obviously bitter taste for many. Opponents decried his Copperhead leanings and warned of the "Rumocracy" to come under a

ABOVE: *Artist's view of Wentworth guests sightseeing from the hotel veranda. (LK)*

ABOVE: *Painted the color of money, the hotel
briefly sported a Nile green coat of paint with
a yellow stripe. (ATH)*

66    WENTWORTH BY THE SEA

Jones administration. Yet Jones was still an important employer in the state, a pillar of the Portsmouth community and a major taxpayer. In one day in 1879 he paid a $5,700 duty in gold to the Portsmouth Custom House for just a small portion of the 400,000 bushels of hops being imported to his brewery from Canada. But all his resources could not buy Jones the gubernatorial seat. He lost the election, deciding perhaps to devote his resources to buying other politicians.

It seems unavoidably symbolic that, a few years after purchasing the Hotel Wentworth, Jones had the exterior painted Nile green, the color of money. Before that, in an initial burst of "extensive repairs," according to newspaper accounts, Jones and Hilton ordered a cleansing coat of paint for every room and frescoed walls in the parlor, dining hall, and rotunda. The colorful handiwork of fresco and stencil craftsmen, like Phillip Butler of Boston, were the height of Victorian fashion, and— the painter's advertisements noted—the painting could disguise cracks and blemishes in the walls and ceilings. Improving on the boxy Wentworth created by Campbell and Chase, Jones added layers of Colonial Revival features. A few details of the ornate ceiling painting, finely crafted wooden paneling, and decorative plaster still survive, mostly in the Rockingham Hotel and in his Maplewood Farm. Yet with a few exceptions, Jones's incredible decorative and architectural work at the Wentworth during two major renovations was either bulldozed or stripped away by a series of owners during the limbo years of the late twentieth century.

Jones's initial improvements included a thirty-by-sixty-foot stable to keep horses available for guests at all times. Ferries and sailboats could tie up to a new floating dock. A new dam on the Little Harbor side allowed swimmers and inexperienced boaters to access what amounted to a private saltwater lake rather than brave the chilly New Hampshire ocean. Hilton introduced steam-driven elevators and a new steam ferry. A Concord coach carriage seating twenty waited to whisk guests from Jones's train in Portsmouth to their luxury accommodations. A Western Union telegraph, and then later a miraculous telephone wire, connected the Wentworth to its sister, the Rockingham Hotel,

TOP: *The Sinclair House, built of brick by Frank Jones for his daughter, employed a similar roof and tower design. It is today an apartment house on Middle Street. (JDR)*

BOTTOM: *The Jones family's Maplewood mansion is also divided into apartments today. Again the signature tower is evident. This detail shows only a small portion of the expansive grounds with stables. (JDR)*

FISHING FROM THE ROCKS

ABOVE: *Fishing from the rocks at the Wentworth in the 1880s. (LK)*

OPPOSITE TOP: *A rare view of the Wentworth summer orchestra and dancers during the Victorian era. Dances, or hops, were popular from the opening days of the hotel. (LK)*

OPPOSITE BELOW: *The accuracy of this illustration from the 1880s can be determined by comparing it to the earlier photograph of the dining area during the Campbell era. This drawing shows the identical chairs, columns, lighting, and beam structure of the room in the 1870s. (LK)*

in town. As soon as they were available, seven high-tech outdoor electrical arc lights cast a flickering futuristic glow for the first time in New Castle. When the lights came on in July 1880, a *Journal* reporter quipped: "With the seven electric lights so well posted around the Wentworth, it is impossible for Stephen to kiss Chloe on the sly within a mile of Newcastle."

Of all the fancy new features at the Wentworth, none was more welcome to the Victorian traveler than the marvelous water closet. To provide the first flush toilets, even just a few for shared use on each hotel floor, Frank Hilton needed much more water. The spring down by the harbor became the source. This costly new sanitation system received as much coverage in Hilton's first Wentworth brochure as did the famous view. Yet in the nineteenth century, despite the great attention paid to sanitation, the outflow of the hotel sewage system flushed directly into Little Harbor. From there the twice-daily tides carried the effluent across New Castle's western shoreline and out into the great blue toilet.

For drinking water, Hilton created a reservoir adjacent to the hotel on four new acres of land purchased for $1,500 from Israel and Ellen Fletcher. Still more water was needed. A temporary aqueduct system was rigged up to pipe water from Portsmouth, past the old Benning Wentworth mansion and along Little Harbor, past Campbell Cottage and over to the Wentworth. Sarah and Charles Campbell signed an agreement allowing Jones to carry the water across their spit of land below the hotel. No longer an owner or manager, Charles became a night watchman and winter caretaker at the Wentworth, a job he held for the rest of his life. But the new water wasn't enough. A year later Hilton & Company hired drillers to cut through the ledge, finally tapping a source of fresh water at 250 feet that reportedly brought in 2,500 barrels a day.

Next the hotel's shoebox design of Erasmus Mansfield got a serious makeover. The Hotel Wentworth that we recognize today took shape between the close of F. W. Hilton &

Company's first season in fall 1879, and the reopening in summer 1880. Frank Jones pulled out all the stops, adding another story to the main building, attaching three distinctive towers, and topping the imposing new structure with a red curved, or mansard, roof. Extensive renovations doubled the length of the front of the hotel to 160 feet, increasing the hotel's capacity. Italian-style awnings sprouted from every window and banners fluttered from poles high atop the three towers.

A newspaper report in October 1879 captured the beginning of the renovation:

> Outside this fine establishment in Newcastle is a scene of busy activity. Mr. Joseph R. Holmes, with a gang of thirty men, is engaged in blasting ledges, building cellar walls, and laying out grounds for lawn tennis, etc. Easterly of the main house extends a cellar wall eighty feet in length, the foundation for the extension of the dining hall; while on the western side are being erected, the walls for the extension of the main house. This work is being done in the most substantial manner. The frame for the new part is daily expected to arrive…

Holmes had previously won the contract to build the New Castle bridge in 1874. Now the structural frames were built in distant Waterville, Maine, and shipped south to New Castle to Holmes's waiting crew in an early version of prefab construction. The blasting of the "unsightly" rocky area showed a modern determination, unlike that of Campbell and Chase, to conform the land to the will of the owner. A small army of "planterers" under W. J. Frase, according to the newspaper, had made marked changes in the layout of the hotel grounds. The creation of the tennis courts in full view of a hundred hotel windows demonstrated Hilton's understanding that wealthy guests wanted more diversions suited to their advanced social status. First tennis, and soon after golfing and yachting, came to define the country-club lifestyle that would usher in a new century. More than $40,000 had already been spent on improvements in 1879 according to one fall report, with no end in sight. By December 1880, the cost was estimated at $100,000.

OPPOSITE TOP: *A stark close-up of the hotel while it was painted green. Note the awnings and original electric lights. (ATH)*

OPPOSITE BOTTOM: *Tennis and golf were popular during Frank Jones's era and tournament results against other hotel teams were avidly reported in the local newspapers. This photograph appeared in a brochure after Jones's death, but may have been taken much earlier during the "green" years. (ATH)*

THE·WENTWORTH

We have a detailed eyewitness account of the interior of the renovated hotel from an 1880 article in the *Granite State Monthly*. The writer is most impressed by the elevator just off the main entrance. Glancing into the telegraph office, the gentlemen's waiting area, and the reception room, the writer steps through an arched corridor into the parlor in the middle of the house with windows on either side. The parlor, like the rest of the hotel, is ornamented in dark ash and maple paneling. An imposing fireplace of inlaid walnut is decorated in a unique Japanese pattern, unlike anything else seen in the state of New Hampshire. Beyond the parlor, wide doors on either end of the corridor lead onto the veranda. Crossing the hall, visitors enter a five-hundred-seat theater, lit by gas and electricity, with a stage in the center for concerts and plays with dressing rooms on either side.

Back at the office, now turning right, the visitor enters an immense dining room, 120 by 42 feet, lighted by sixteen

ABOVE: *Albee's 1884* History of New Castle *included this romantic illustration of the hotel showing the large ledge, later broken up. (JA)*

windows and encircled by a seemingly endless sideboard. A room for children and their nurses is off to the side; opposite them is the gentlemen's reading area and a sitting room. The reporter is especially impressed by the working area of the Wentworth, a place never seen by visitors, yet spacious and clean and filled with laborsaving machinery. The service area is nearly as expansive as the parlor, with a separate dish pantry thirty-five feet long. There, according to the reporter, the first dish washing machine ever invented was in operation. The kitchen is large and airy enough to keep separate dishes from exchanging odors and far enough from the dining area to isolate the smells of cooking. A large modern ice refrigerator stands against one wall.

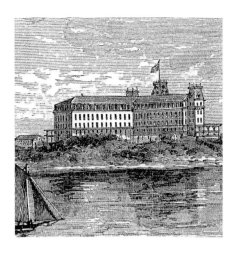

Taking an elevator to the sleeping area, the writer is impressed by the "beauty of equality" in the two hundred rooms. They are generally of the same size, equipped with black walnut Queen Anne-style furniture, and all have a view.

"There is not a poor room or a back room in the house," the reporter notes with obvious amazement. He strolls the veranda that nearly encircles the hotel, commenting on the view of the ocean, the view of the bay, the copse of pine trees. He drinks in the salt sea air and walks down the three terraced lawns where visitors play croquet and lawn tennis. He wanders below the bluff to a crescent-shaped little beach of pure white sand and looks down the long wooden piers. By the time the stars come out and the cool island breeze picks up, and John Braham's twenty-piece orchestra begins to play, this reporter, too, is fully enchanted.

Frank Hilton knew how to please his wealthy clientele, many of whom stayed for an entire season. It was the extra touches that mattered—the billiard room, the bathing houses, the miniature steamer for children that chugged around the warmer salt lake. Hilton contracted with Mr. Urch, who owned the toll bridge, for use of a "marine bicycle." He instituted athletic competitions, another longtime Wentworth tradition, including sprints, walking races, and rowing and swimming races. Hilton had the great sense to retain John Braham of Boston and his orchestra for the entire season, adding a soundtrack to the elegant summer. The steamship *Gypsy* was ready for tours. Two converted whaleboats were available for fishing parties. Horses

ABOVE: *Wentworth Hotel from the side showing the back* L *dining area that made the hotel much larger, even from the beginning, than it appeared from the front. (ATH)*

THE "WENTWORTH," NEWCASTLE, N. H., AND ITS ATTRACTIONS AS A SUMMER RESORT.

were groomed at all times. Carriage drivers were prompt and neatly dressed. Hundreds of anonymous workers were seen but not heard. All the little details combined into a feeling of opulence that telegraphed to guests the message that they were very special and important people who deserved every pampered moment, no matter what the cost.

For all his management skills, Hilton was also the hotel's first real marketing agent. He knew the value of advertising and of public relations. One of his first acts on renovating the hotel was to hold a lunch for local hack and ferry drivers, who he knew, would spread the word among their customers that the Wentworth and the Rockingham were the best accommodations around. Though he was unafraid to hire the best dance band from Boston or the best carpenter from Maine, he knew when to hire locally. He also knew when to advertise locally, running a whopping eight-inch-tall ad in the *Portsmouth Chronicle* throughout the 1880 summer season. The artfully worded ad hit every marketing highlight—the view, the food, the orchestra, the renovations, the furniture, the local attractions, the fun and games, the sanitation. Just two hours from Boston by train, the hotel was now closer to Portsmouth (three miles instead of four) in a convenient new calculation. Hilton was even careful to mention that his inland saltwater swimming and boating area was warmer than the frigid Atlantic Ocean offered by his beachside competitors.

The Wentworth advertised nationally, apparently with much success. In a rare interview on September 20th, 1881 with the *Portsmouth Chronicle*, manager Frank Hilton spoke candidly about his wealthy guests. Unlike other hotels that saw the same guests year to year, he suggested that the first wave of Wentworth visitors were coming from greater distances and had never been to the coast or even to New England before. The guest list, he said, included visitors from nearly every state in the Union and from Canada. These were often businessmen, Hilton suggested, men unafraid of travel and who worked very hard in major cities during the year. In summer they migrated east with their families in order to rest, to breathe the healthy air, to be pampered, and to grow stronger over the summer in order to face

OPPOSITE: *Revealing details of the Wentworth are often best seen in early illustrations, as in this full-page collage. Included here is a snapshot of actors on the hotel stage and of cabins in the bathing area. (RMC)*

another high-stress year in a smog-filled city. Patrons from Louisville, Cincinnati, Chicago, and St. Louis dominated the hotel register, Hilton said proudly, and attributed their patronage to "a judicious system of advertising." Hilton told the *Chronicle:* "These are men of wealth and refinement. They want the best service, and are willing to pay for it … Their entire families seem to appreciate the atmosphere at the Wentworth, and leave it with regret."

Local businessmen then, as now, knew the magnifying economic value of first-time visitors, especially to a state that few Americans were aware had a coastline at all. Frank Jones's advertising dollars, combined with the growing fame of Hampton Beach and the legendary Isles of Shoals, were turning the region into a serious destination point for summer visitors. The resulting tourist dollars had a healthy impact on the economy of Portsmouth and the region. Local vendors maintained the grounds, did the laundry, served the food, delivered the ice and farm products, renovated the building, managed the small flotilla of sailboats, and did every other skilled and menial job that kept the hotel operating.

All of this, Hilton noted in his interview, cost money. Asked if the successful season at the hotel had required a great outlay of cash, Hilton responded like the highly stressed manager he was:

> Yes. You would think so if you had to pay the bills. For instance, our beef bill alone amounts to over four thousand dollars, while we paid over sixteen hundred dollars for the single article of butter. The pay roll of help in the house, including boatmen, was over ten thousand dollars. Yes, it takes a trifle of money to run a hotel of this character, but I am happy to say that every bill is paid, and we have enough left to put in our ice for next year.

A member of the local Board of Trade, a forerunner of the chamber of commerce, noted that Frank Jones never made a dollar that didn't benefit Portsmouth. Others might suggest that those who extracted dollars from Frank Jones worked hard to get them. He was not known for a single large philanthropic act. Still, in July of the 1880 season, the Board of Trade honored

ABOVE: *A carriage arrives at the expanding Wentworth. The extensive addition is visible from this perspective. (ATH)*

Jones and Hilton with a formal party at the Wentworth. Male dignitaries feasted, toasted, smoked cigars, and praised one another until midnight. The menu for the event survives, and offers a taste of the times:

Little Neck Clams
Soup
Clam Chowder, Mock Turtle
Broiled Kennebec Salmon, Anchovy Sauce
Broiled Leg of English Mutton, Caper Sauce
Roast Rhode Island Green Ducks
Roast Sirloin of Beef
Sliced Tomatoes, Cucumbers
Galantine of Turkey, Lobster Salad
Sweetbreads, Larded with Green Peas
Macaroni Baked, à la Crème
Roman Punch
Yellow Legs, Snipes, Philadelphia Squabs
Saratoga Fried Potatoes
English Plum Pudding, Champagne Jelly
Chocolate Russe, Crèam [sic] Puffs, Bananas, Oranges
Peaches, Nuts, Lemon Ice Cream, Raisins
Blackberries, Watermelons
Coffee

The rich diet, the stress of managing two world-class hotels, and the ravages of war were taking their toll on Frank W. Hilton. Following the successful 1881 season during which many of the guests booked a second summer in advance, he laid out a plan to add more rooms to the hotel. He struggled to solve the ongoing water problem and paid off all the outstanding summer bills. Then, with his work done, on January 19, 1882, Captain Frank W. Hilton died, age forty. Although he appeared healthy, the newspaper noted, he had long been an invalid, suffering from heart and liver ailments.

Hilton's obituary outlined his impressive Civil War record and his lengthy struggle with malaria. Under Hilton, one eulogy reported with kind exaggeration, the Wentworth had grown from a rustic hotel on a hill into one of the finest resorts in all of America.

# Summer Playground

A favorite pastime of Wentworth by the Sea guests in the late twentieth century was dressing up like guests from the nineteenth century, the women in hourglass gowns and the men in top hats. Mid-twentiety-century owners James and Margaret Smith were fascinated by the genteel image of their grand hotel in the Gay Nineties-era of Frank Jones. It was a case of the Smiths trying to keep up with the Joneses.

This nostalgic longing for the sensible, mannered past came from generations weary of war and accelerating social and technological change. As Americans in the second half of the twentieth century adapted to the space race and rock 'n' roll, Wentworth summer guests imagined a time before airplanes, Univac computers and weapons of mass destruction. They saw, through rose-colored glasses, a simple, elegant, opulent time when the living was easy and the world made sense—at least to those of wealth and social standing.

For the next two decades, from the death of Frank Hilton in 1882 to his own death in 1902, Frank Jones worked to keep his hotels among the finest on the East Coast. His "new wealth" customers too were playing a form of dress-up, acting out their Americanized version of an aristocracy drawn from a mix of European cultures. But Jones was also running a very modern hotel, the forerunner of a five-star resort, good enough even for the president of the United States.

The visit by President Chester A. Arthur in September 1882 put Portsmouth in a festive mood. The ship *Tallapoosa*, with the

ABOVE: *President Chester A. Arthur stopped by the Wentworth and the Rockingham.* (LIB)

OPPOSITE: *A rare group photo of workers building the dining room addition in 1896.* (RMC)

U.S. Secretary of the Navy aboard, steamed into the lower harbor and shot off a display of fireworks to greet the visiting Chief Executive. After military formalities and a twenty-one-gun salute from the shipyard early the next morning, the president and his entourage breakfasted at the Wentworth Hotel in New Castle. The president had been Frank Jones's colleague when both had served in the U.S. House of Representatives just a few years earlier. Arthur had assumed the mantle after the assassination of James Garfield the year before, but he did not shrink from meeting openly with the public.

After breakfast and a quick visit to the Rockingham Hotel to see his friend Frank Jones, the president toured the New Hampshire coast in the hotel's six-horse carriage. Eschewing tight security, the chief executive rode in the open air sitting next to the driver. After a quick late-summer tour of the beaches of Rye, the coach turned at Little Boar's Head in Hampton and trotted back. According to a newspaper report, the president was very pleased by the view from the Wentworth. Jones, in an era untainted by political correctness, offered to give the president a free parcel of land in New Castle if he wanted to build a summer cottage on his favorite spot.

Other presidents had made the Portsmouth visit. George Washington started it in 1789 when he stayed almost four days, taking tea with his friend John Langdon and visiting the mother of his secretary, Tobias Lear, along with Michael Wentworth, who had married the widow of Benning Wentworth. Washington remarked in his journal about the attractive women of Portsmouth who huddled around him at a fancy-dress ball. John Quincy Adams, James Monroe, James Polk, Benjamin Harrison, Ulysses S. Grant, Benjamin Taft, and Harry Truman made whistle-stop tours. New Hampshire's own Franklin Pierce, who, like orator Daniel Webster had trained as a young lawyer in Portsmouth, visited often after his unhappy presidency. Every modern candidate has campaigned in the region, and some slept at the Wentworth. But only three presidential winners reportedly stayed at the Wentworth—Herbert Hoover, Franklin Roosevelt, and Richard Nixon. No documentation exists to date and none were president at the time of their visit. Both presidents Bush used the Portsmouth air base as a stopping point en route to the family compound at Kennebunkport, Maine. Politicians still crowd the region in a tradition that continues every four years during New Hampshire's first-in-the-nation presidential primary.

Even a whistle-stop visit by President Arthur enchanted locals and indicated that Portsmouth was more than a faded colonial capital, and proved, once again, that Frank Jones was a political heavyweight. The visit also affixed the presidential seal, albeit symbolically, to both of Jones's hotels, transforming a vacation outing into a historic event with unlimited marketing potential. Wentworth visits by two more presidents and friends of Jones were rumored but did not come to pass. Grover Cleveland chose to visit Jones instead at his hotel in Sorrento in Maine. William McKinley, whom Jones said he had lunched with 150 to 200 times while in the U.S. Congress, was assassinated in 1901.

President Chester Arthur's visit was also a feather in the cap of Jones's new manager, George T. Thompson, who needed to prove he could fill F. W. Hilton's well-polished shoes. It was Thompson who rode along in the coach during the president's tour of the New Hampshire coast. Thompson had cut his teeth in the White Mountain hotel trade with his father and come up through the Jones empire as a ticket taker in the Portsmouth station of the tycoon's Eastern Railroad. Thompson held on to the reins only three years before he was forced to retire due to illness, but his brief tenure contains a few memorable moments in the history of the hotel. The newspaper gave Thompson the usual vote of confidence as heir to the late Frank Hilton. But there appears, between the lines, the growing understanding that the reputation of the man who managed the prestigious Wentworth and the Rockingham could have an impact on the growing tourism trade in a region known for its rocky economy as well as its rocky shores.

"Nature has been lavish in attractions around our city," the *Chronicle* editorialized upon Thompson's hiring in 1882, "and the manner in which our summer visitors are to be entertained is a concern of no small import to all our people."

ABOVE: *The Wentworth maintained its own printing press. Scores of daily menus survive and show the changing fare of the hotel's always bountiful meals. Two of the stock cover designs are shown here. (ATH)*

The papers followed the hotel news in soap opera detail, even naming the new coachmen, the new telegraph operator and the new summer barber. A Boston news report mentioned that W. S. Patterson, Jones's private German landscape gardener, was hard at work on the undulating lawn outside the "already colossal Wentworth," which was to be "indefinitely extended." We know by report that the streets were lined, as was the fashion, in newly planted maple trees similar to those Frank Jones had planted along the road to his Portsmouth mansion on Maplewood Avenue. A planting of Norway spruce failed, however, when a hundred of them succumbed to drought. When the Wentworth gardener ordered an excess of flowers, coachloads of local women were only too happy to cart them home for free. The Wentworth, summer playground for the distant rich, was becoming a destination for the local community as well.

Nothing mixed tourists and townies like the frequent summer "hops," a tradition begun with enormous success under Charles Campbell and formalized under Frank Hilton with bandmaster John Braham. The music wafting across the island, supported by a healthy dose of newspaper advertising, brought short-stay visitors in droves. The hotel became so populated during the initial year of musical entertainment that one eyewitness referred to the crowded conditions as "a cot by the sea." A newspaper report in the 1890s suggests that as many as five hundred bicycles from local visitors covered the lawn of the hotel during one summer concert. It became necessary at one point, as the Wentworth expanded, to ban those not registered at the hotel from attending the sometimes sweltering dances. Drop-in guests willing to pay for lodging often found the Wentworth full and had to be transferred to the Rockingham by carriage after the festivities ended at night. Before the ban, some locals with the proper means and attire joined in; other Wentworth watchers merely gazed at the elaborate costumes of the lady dancers and dreamed of joining a world far beyond their means.

Although guests were sometimes reluctant to dance, preferring to enjoy the twenty-piece orchestra, the new bandleader, Henry J. Harlow, held a dozen hops during the summer of '82.

OPPOSITE: *Visitors could even dance to the hotel's theme song, released on sheet music in 1892. Boston orchestras and dance bands played throughout the summer from the Campbell era to the Smith era. (JDR)*

# THE WENTWORTH.

A New Dance by EUGENE A. BOURNIQUE.

Music by FRED. L. RYDER.

INTRODUCTION. Tempo di Mazurka.

The band also provided, in July and August alone, 108 concerts, racking up a musical total for the summer season of 216 hours and 40 minutes. Besides acting as house band at the Wentworth, Harlow's popular group played the evolving summer hotel circuit, drawing overflow crowds to the Oceanic and the Appledore on the Isles of Shoals, to Foss Beach in Rye, and to the Portsmouth Music Hall.

Harlow, a well-respected Bostonian, clearly saw dance music as a lesser art, preferring to showcase newer and more complex music when possible. He was admittedly perturbed to discover that the children of the hotel's privileged summer guests thought nothing of running up and requesting the polished orchestra to play "Dancing in the Barn." In one incident, Harlow reported to the newspaper, "a small boy dressed in short velvet pants, silk stockings, fancy jacket, nobby hat and stylish sash" bounced onto the stage during a formal concert in pursuit of a butterfly. Afraid that the urchin might put his foot through the bass drum, the bandleader hoisted him over the railing by his pants and coat and back into the public area.

"Look here!" the child threatened Harlow, "You had better not get us boys down on you."

Ever genial, Harlow noted, manager Thompson quickly found ways to entertain "us boys" without offending either them

or their parents while salvaging the dignity of his band. It was Frank Jones's policy and Thompson's mission to keep everyone at the hotel happy, including the very young. According to Harlow, a guest once asked Frank Jones why he went to "foolish expense" to turn the back harbor into a swimming and boating pond for children.

"Why, don't you know," Jones reportedly responded, "that little boys and girls make men and women, and that ten years from now they will remember with pleasure the little pond and steamer back of the Wentworth and will be more likely to visit us in the future? And what do we live for, if it is not to make all the happiness we can?"

In October 1882 the *Portsmouth Journal* reported that a party of Boston men had a diver searching for buried treasure at New Castle near the Wentworth Hotel. The search party had been quietly at work dragging the waters for months by the bridge at the entrance to Little Harbor. The group reportedly held a hundred-year-old document "whose authenticity is undoubted." Details of the treasure hunt filtered out to the public through the newspapers for three years as the search continued. The treasure map, reports said, had been discovered in the lining of a vest belonging to an elderly man who had died at New Castle. In 1883 a professional dowser from Belfast, Maine, helped in the

ABOVE: *A panoramic detail from across Little Harbor shows the large number of outbuildings and cottages connected to the hotel. At its peak, the resort included nearly 300 acres in New Castle and Rye. (CAM)*

fruitless search for what was now defined as three chests of gold, a barrel of silver, and a box of coins.

It wasn't until the fall of 1884 that a more detailed and skeptical account of the treasure hunt appeared in the *New York Mail*, and was promptly reprinted in the Portsmouth paper. A methodical three-year search had yielded nothing, and according to the reporter, the owners of the treasure map told their story reluctantly. The harrowing tale, in a nutshell, goes like this:

An unnamed clergyman from England at some distant time in the past planned to transport a considerable fortune to do God's will in the New World. The crew of the ship, learning of the treasure, put the clergyman ashore on the barren Isles of Shoals with only a goat for a companion. Leaving the Isles, the pirate ship was hit by a severe storm and the crew was forced to take shelter in nearby Little Harbor. For reasons unknown, the pirates buried the treasure and made a map that somehow ended up in the hands of a schoolteacher who was taken sick and nursed by a family in Maine. But the teacher died, and on his deathbed was moved to reveal to his benefactors the location of the treasure. A map sewn into his coat lining, he confessed, showed the spot near a bridge at Great Island in New Hampshire.

A man from Melrose, Massachusetts, inherited the alleged map by marrying a descendant of the family that had nursed the dying teacher. While the backstory was as vague as the many pirate legends of the New England coast, the directions were seductively specific. According to the chart, the treasure was located "25 rods below the bridge, 20 rods below Black Point at low water where there is a rock 3 x 4 feet, with the formation of a windowsill on top."

Unfortunately for the diggers, at least three bridges had spanned the entrance to Little Harbor between New Castle and Rye, and the map did not specify at which bridge or in what era the treasure was buried. The salvage crew uncovered an area sixteen feet deep and fifty feet square apparently without locating a single artifact. But seacoast tales of buried treasure, no matter how improbable, never die. A single bar of silver reportedly found on Smuttynose Island prior to the Revolution, though the discovery has never been substantiated, has fueled local treasure

OPPOSITE TOP: *A view of the gentleman's area under the management of W. K. Hill shows the carved wooden fireplace mantel that was rebuilt in 2003. The dome in the background has survived intact and is now in the hotel dining room. (ATH)*

OPPOSITE BOTTOM: *A nineteenth-century passion for orderliness here indicates that hundreds of guests could dine in perfect harmony in the massive room. (ATH)*

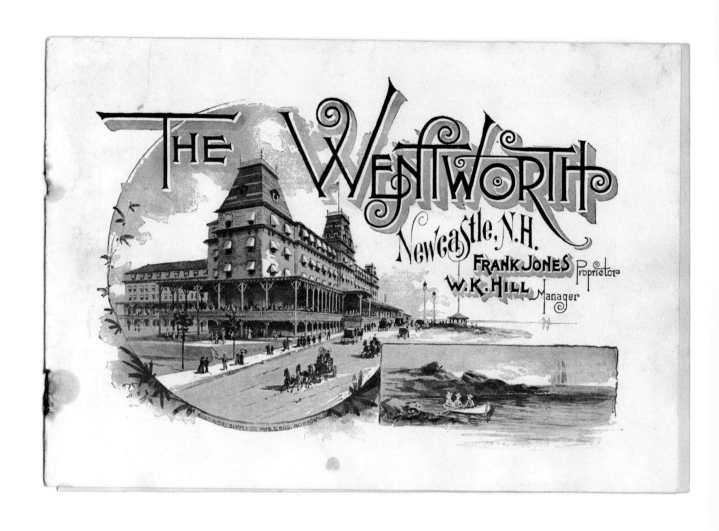

ABOVE: *The cover of one of many elaborate brochures published under manager Hill, a master of advertising and public relations. It is rare for Jones's name to appear so boldly in the advertising. (RMC)*

hunters for centuries. Just recently, tracing the vague legend of Blackbeard the pirate, a film crew from *The History Channel* used ground-penetrating radar and a robotic drill to bore into solid granite at the Isles of Shoals—again to no avail.

The years of the treasure search coincide precisely with the research and publication of John Albee's *History of New Castle*, which appeared in 1884. Copies of the book, according to the newspaper, were "gratuitously forwarded to patrons of the Wentworth." Hotel guests already tracking the buried treasure story, now had a comprehensive and portable guide to the rich history and lore of New Castle, similar to walking guides already available for Portsmouth, the Hamptons, the Yorks and the Isles of Shoals.

Around this same time, Thompson issued a twelve-page advertising brochure that the newspaper praised as "the best hotel circular we have yet seen." In an early example of direct-mail marketing, 10,000 pamphlets were posted to potential patrons. Rare, fragile paper flyers have survived from the opening of the Wentworth a decade before, but Thompson's piece offered unprecedented consumer information, including a schematic of all four floors of the hotel with prices listed by the day, the week, and the month. Advertising continued to emphasize the hotel's elevation, ventilation, and drainage among its healthy assets. Sewage, potential guests were told, was discreetly removed to a distance of two thousand feet where the aggressive local tides carried away the effluent.

It was also under Thompson that the Hotel Wentworth briefly turned green and gained its distinctive red roof. A coat of oil applied the following year to the Nile green paint gave the hotel on the hill an exotic appearance. After the horses pulling the Wentworth coach bolted during a trip to Portsmouth, causing a major accident on Deer Street, Thompson purchased the famous Tally-Ho coach with its six horses in English harness for sixty-three hundred dollars. It was Thompson who added fifty new rooms and another $175,000 of Jones money was reportedly allocated for an enormous makeover.

The hotel, according to architect Fred N. Footman, would be extended to 646 feet and encircled by verandas twenty feet wide. The central tower, the largest of five, would include a

TOP: *The small building and pen appear in many hotel ads, but their use was a mystery until recently. (ATH)*

BOTTOM: *A rarely seen sketch purchased by a Wentworth ephemera collector indicates that the area was used as a deer pen under manager Hill. (LK)*

ABOVE: *Sports became fashionable for the wealthy toward the end of the nineteenth century. The Wentworth offered the finest facilities for boating, baseball, golfing, riding, swimming, tennis, and bicycling. Posed here is the New Castle Tennis and Outing Club. (RMC)*

*The renovated Wentworth on opening week in the
summer of 2003 looking from the Roosevelt Room into
the lobby through a surviving doorway.
Photograph by W. Garrett Scholes*

7664

OPPOSITE: *Scores of postcards document the twentieth century evolution of the hotel from the horse and carriage era to motorcars. (RMC)*

ABOVE: *Avid collectors continue to unearth every imaginable souvenir from the Wentworth's first hundred years. (PER)*

LEFT: *One of a complete set of inscribed silver-plated coffee, tea and cocoa servers presented to Sarah and Charles Campbell by the staff and guests of Wentworth House during the end of its first season in 1874. The set remains in the Campbell family. (PER)*

The Wentwo

w Castle, N. H.

OVERLEAF TOP: *A turn-of-the-twentieth century double-wide colorized postcard showing awnings on all windows. (ATH)*

OVERLEAF BOTTOM: *Two aerial views showing the hotel during the Smith era (left) and today as designed by TMS Architects and owned by Ocean Properties, with the rerouted New Castle road . (photos by Ralph Morang)*

ABOVE: *The Friends of the Wentworth gather in the rain to form a human chain around the endangered Wentworth by the Sea just prior to its salvation. (SN)*

RIGHT: *A view from the top looking onto the battered hotel during its limbo years in the 1990s. (SG)*

ABOVE: *About three quarters of Frank Jones's Colonial Revival addition was demolished in the late twentieth century (SG)*

LEFT: *The restored Wentworth, October, 2003. (PER)*

*In the reconstructed hotel, TMS architects took care to preserve a few original features. Shown above is the ballroom stage (OP)and at right the original doorway, photograph by W. Garrett Scholes*

stairway eighteen feet wide. A new "saloon" 50 by 170 feet would lead to the dining room, complete with a great fountain and two immense fireplaces. One hundred and fifty of the sleeping rooms would have their own parlors with fireplace.

The whole plan was served up in a detailed model displayed in the gentlemen's reading room at the Rockingham Hotel. Fire, illness, and another hotel, however, distracted the ale tycoon's attentions from the Wentworth and delayed reconstruction. The real problem with Footman's plan, according to architectural historian Richard Candee, was the timeline. The extensive redesign required a full year of work, and the loss of a summer's income was a ticket even Jones could not afford.

Footman, a native of nearby Somersworth, New Hampshire, did design Frank Jones's elaborate summer home in Sorrento, Maine. A number of his ideas for the Wentworth, taken piecemeal from the master plan, were incorporated into the hotel over the next two decades. Another architect, Jesse B. Edwards, is credited with making renovations to the Wentworth under Jones. Edwards also worked on the Jones brewery and on Maplewood Farm, Jones's Portsmouth mansion.

In 1884 the Rockingham Hotel, sister to the Wentworth, burned. Frank Jones turned his attentions to rebuilding the stately brick structure—it survives today with some of its dark wood paneling and even a number of ornate painted ceilings intact. The four well-known sculpted Rockingham lions that guard the entrance, installed in 1872, managed to survive the fire. How Jones rebounded from the loss of the Rockingham— his home away from home and the symbol of his rise from poverty to power—is a case study in his uncanny ability to profit even from adversity.

In short, the insurance companies that held the policy on the Rockingham refused to pay up. Even after making Jones wait months for an investigation, they did not settle for the $50,000 they owed him. Perhaps they were suspicious of the mysterious fire that had demolished his National Hotel back in 1877. A dispute arose and was settled in Jones's favor by an independent team. Still the insurance companies would not budge. Jones pulled on his legislative strings and got the State of New

ABOVE: *When the Rockingham hotel burned in 1884, Jones turned his attention temporarily to rebuilding an even grander version. Manager Hill continued the practice of "co-marketing" the two seacoast New Hampshire hotels and of promoting the region as a major destination for visitors from distant states. In later years, Jones spent much of his time at another of his hotels, in Sorrento, Maine, where he kept a grand cottage. (ATH)*

Hampshire to pass a law requiring that, except in the case of fraud, insurance companies pay the total amount due. In protest, the insurance companies refused to honor claims in New Hampshire, hoping to frighten businessmen and taxpayers into rescinding the law. To fill the void Frank Jones himself went into the insurance business. The Granite State Fire Insurance Company, active into the late twentieth century, was formed in 1886. Its offices were originally located in the posh new Rockingham Hotel that reopened the same year.

The year the Rockingham burned, Jones was busy expanding his real estate holdings in the then unlikely vacation state of Florida, which he believed had great potential for growth in the coming twentieth century. He was also heavily invested in the expanding telephone industry, on the verge of owning his own bank, president of the Boston & Maine Railroad, and preparing to launch a new hotel, the Sorrento, on Frenchman's Bay in Maine. But he never forgot the Wentworth, and solved problem after problem in typical Jonesian fashion. When the hotel needed more ice for its summer refrigerators, for example, he bought land farther down Wentworth Road, created a pond, and installed a commercial ice-cutting operation, not far from the site of the Ice House Restaurant today. Instead of leasing fine horses for his carriages, Jones bought his own mighty teams that could be seen grazing off-season on Peirce Island in Portsmouth. Rather than rely on local farmers, Jones purchased eleven acres behind the hotel and installed his own vegetable gardens.

Most impressive was Jones's attitude about the advent of electrical power. Inspired by Thomas Edison's first experiment, lighting up a few blocks in New York City with direct current in 1882, Jones was among the earliest to install a private generator at his mansion in Portsmouth. Soon after, as it became possible to generate power beyond the half-mile limit dictated by direct current, Jones built his own power plant. Workers shoveling coal into boilers at Jones's power plant on Islington Street made steam that turned large dynamos. By the 1890s, Jones's private power plant provided electricity to his brewery, his home, his downtown office buildings, the Rockingham, and all the way to the Wentworth in New Castle.

While Jones was undaunted by hundreds of such projects running simultaneously, another of his generals capitulated. George Thompson took ill and was replaced in 1886 by William K. Hill, the manager who would outlive Jones. Over the next decade and half, under Hill's firm hand, the Wentworth held its place as one of the most extensive seaside resorts in what was becoming a crowded field. The Passaconnaway in York and the Champernowne in Kittery were now visible from the hotel veranda. Rail service, and soon the addition of electric trolleys, was making the beaches of New Hampshire, Maine, and the Massachusetts North Shore accessible to low-income families and day-trippers. As the industry expanded, so did the Wentworth.

The last decade of the nineteenth century found the Wentworth settling in to the business of being a hotel. In fact, without the history-making peace treaty of 1905, it might have become simply another New Hampshire hotel. Frank Jones was in his sixties now and spending more time traveling and enjoying his wealth. That left William K. Hill with two opulent hotels to run, each with its own extensive staff, plus the Wentworth grounds and seaside facilities, coach lines, electrical service, food, laundry, cleaning, entertainment, publicity, and administration to oversee. But mostly manager Hill's job was to fill beds. Though itinerant guests were on the rise, the hotel still survived on advance bookings from wealthy patrons who stayed the entire summer season. The manager often traveled the eastern United States off-season, singing the praises of his two Portsmouth hotels. It worked. The Wentworth's reputation, even in southern states, was considered all but unbeatable as the twentieth century approached.

The Wentworth had it all—new docks, new stables with forty Thoroughbreds, even a new ladies billiard room. A new seven-ton boiler was so big that it had to be delivered to the hotel by river on a flat-bottomed gundalow. Skilled Italian workers were busy "concreting" paths around the hotel and along the bathing area.

The Wentworth's reputation for sports as well as luxury was also growing. The annual lawn tennis tournament, begun in 1881, was heavily attended, except during a couple of cold, wet

ABOVE: *Sketch of tennis or badminton players at the back of the hotel near the deer pen.* *(RMC)*

Julys in the 1890s. Guests from nearby resorts competed year after year and rising cash prizes attracted serious sportsmen and -women to an expanding summer circuit. The specially manicured courts cost four hundred dollars to prepare, according to an 1887 account, and the best courts were reserved for the best players. The following year crowds were entertained between sets by a Hungarian Gypsy band. Meanwhile, the evolution of America's newest national pastime required that the hotel create a baseball field. Jones had a diamond built on part of the current golf course so that the hotel team could take on rivals.

Although late among resorts to add golf, Frank Jones did so at last with gusto, leasing thirty acres farther up Wentworth Road, where the modern Wentworth Country Club stands today. Jones installed a nine-hole course and built a classy clubhouse. He had to, as wealthy fans of the popular sport were beginning to select their summer resort based on the quality of its course. When it opened it rated, according to the *Portsmouth Times* (the newspaper was purchased in 1897 by funds loaned to the owner by Jones), as among the finest golf courses in the world. Women players were active, too, though hobbled by elaborate and confining clothing that kept their scores painfully high by modern standards.

Besides its bread-and-butter seasonal residents, the Wentworth needed to attract large groups, preferably ones that would return annually. Jones's own Granite State Insurance Company and Frank Jones Brewery held elaborate events at the close of each year. For two years the Harvard football team opened the season, training on the fields of a private estate nearby.

The local press routinely covered gala events at the Wentworth, detailing the speeches, toasts, guests, fashions, menus, and decorations. Winners of sports tournaments were listed in print. But the lives of hundreds, perhaps thousands, who kept the hotel running through the nineteenth century are all but unknown to history. Portsmouth, at the time, was a melting pot of Italians, Irish, Prussians, Greeks, Scandinavians, Russians, some African-Americans and Chinese and other ethnic groups, all governed largely by families descended for generations from the region's usually British founders. We can assume some worked within the hotel walls, but many employees were apparently imported for the summer from distant points. When a group of tray- and bell-boys attempted a strike in the 1890s, a local source reports, they were all escorted to the departing train to Boston and quickly replaced. Firing and rehiring, the same process Jones had used in his brewery, was the simple solution in a nonunion age. But the cheap labor kettle was beginning to boil over.

One Saturday night Wentworth employees rebelled against William Hill's enforced curfew of workers. What incidents, if any, led to the harsh practice of imprisoning employee staff at night are unknown. On August 6, 1896, a rare report into the world of the hotel's domestic population appeared in the Portsmouth newspaper.

> It seems that some of the help are very restive over the order that locks them into their quarters at ten o'clock and some have several times attempted to injure Mr. Edward Bewley, the special policeman from this city who has been employed at the house to see that the order is obeyed, attempting to fell him by dropping ewers and bowls upon his head.

Anticipating trouble, according to the report, Bewley had hired two special officers to assist him. Trouble arose. The two part-timers spotted the hotel's second headwaiter attempting to drop a barrel onto Mr. Bewley and all three pursued and entered the employee quarters to catch him. When the male workers threatened to murder the policemen, they held the crowd at bay with their revolvers and summoned manager Hill. The head-waiter was captured, even though he had built "a formidable barricade" at the top of the stairs. It was the employee, however, who gave the ultimatum. He ordered Mr. Hill to unlock the doors and dismiss the officers, or all the Wentworth staff would walk out in protest, leaving Mr. Hill to handle 350 guests alone. Hill relented, according to the report. The lock was removed, the officers sent home, and no one was arrested.

Despite trouble with "the help," the Wentworth, then able to accommodate five hundred guests, would grow one more wing thanks to the largesse of the Hon. Frank Jones. Jones, who spent

ABOVE: *Originally, the hotel's extensive fields along the water in Rye were used as much for baseball as for golf. Under Jones and an army of landscapers, the links grew, attracting spirited summer rivalries among other clubs and hotels. (RMC)*

his last dozen summers at his hotel in Sorrento, Maine, was forever on the lookout for features to add to his many hotels. With his wife, Martha, sometimes with his stepdaughter and her family, he frequently visited London, toured Europe and Mexico, took in the hot baths in Arizona, and checked business deals from Florida to Georgia. Their tour of Canada and the Maritimes caused joking speculation that Jones was considering the purchase of Nova Scotia. The Joneses traveled everywhere in style, with regal coaches, a flurry of servants and maids, their own private Pullman car, and a private yacht, the *Ibis*. No longer the ale tycoon, having by now sold his beloved brewery, Jones had gained a new reputation for breeding winning racehorses at his Portsmouth mansion and stables. Jones built his own racing track in nearby Dover. He seemed almost unable to lose money.

In 1897 the Seacoast lost one of its most popular tourist attractions thanks to John Fitzgerald, grandfather of the future president John F. Kennedy. "Honey Fitz," as he was known, led a Massachusetts movement to reclaim *Old Ironsides*, the famous naval ship that had been languishing in Portsmouth Harbor. Cabbed over and turned into a floating dormitory for cadets, the *U.S.S. Constitution* had become a must-see for visitors, who rowed or were ferried to its berth at the Portsmouth Navy Shipyard. But patriotic sentiments were on the rise with the Spanish-American War. Honey Fitz wanted *Old Ironsides* back at her home port near Boston, and had the ancient ship towed past New Castle and on to Charlestown in time for her hundredth anniversary.

In her place came an even stranger tourist attraction. On July 5, 1898, the U.S. auxiliary cruiser *St. Louis* left Santiago, Cuba, with seven hundred captured prisoners of war. Six days later the prison ship steamed into Portsmouth Harbor and deposited the men on Seavey Island, at the Navy Yard. Haggard and hungry, the men were transferred by barge to the hastily constructed Camp Long. Blocked by palisades on two sides and the swift-flowing river all around, the prisoners were in full view of passing tourist boats. Frank Jones himself joined a group of wealthy Wentworth guests who cruised out to watch the arrival of the Spanish prisoners. Guarded by marines stationed along the

OPPOSITE TOP: *In 1898 summer tourists flocked to see the Spanish prisoners encamped on Seavey's Island where the Portsmouth Naval Prison now stands. The Wentworth's own ferry conducted special viewing tours. Here the prisoners of war wash their dishes in the Piscataqua River. (PPL)*

OPPOSITE BOTTOM: *During most of Jones's tenure, "Old Ironsides" was docked at the navy yard in Kittery. Cabbed over to house young mariners, the famed U.S.S. Constitution reached its nadir in Portsmouth Harbor. Oliver Wendell Holmes, who composed the poem that saved the ship, reportedly stayed at either the Wentworth or the Rockingham during this period. Old Ironsides was removed from Portsmouth Harbor in 1877 to Charleston, Massachusetts as shown here in this early postcard. (JDR)*

island with Gatling guns every fifty feet, the prisoners waved to tourists, who "Kodaked" the moment, snapping photos of the men as they washed their dishes in the river, fished, and staged mock bullfights to the great delight of onlookers and the media. The local newspaper issued instructions on where best to view the prisoners from the third New Castle bridge. A souvenir photo pamphlet sponsored by a local bank quickly appeared.

It was a strange reaction, perhaps, for a town that earlier in the war had feared reprisals by the Spanish fleet. For a time, after the sinking of the *U.S.S. Maine*, Portsmouth Harbor had been mined against possible invasion by sea. Then came a decisive victory in the Philippines at Manila Bay by Commodore George Dewey under the cry "Remember the *Maine!*" The Spanish fleet had been effectively destroyed by Dewey, who himself had strong ties to the region. He had served at the Navy Yard during the Civil War and married Susan Goodwin, daughter of New Hampshire governor Ichabod Goodwin of Portsmouth.

Though technically a prisoner, captured Spanish Admiral Cuervera Pascuel Cervera was allowed to roam the region as he negotiated the release of his officers and men, traveling back and forth from New Hampshire to Annapolis. While in Portsmouth, he stayed at the Rockingham Hotel. The public immediately took to the distinguished bearded man in his white suit with a cane and treated Cervera like a superstar.

When the admiral visited the Wentworth Hotel in August, he was so mobbed by admiring ladies, the newspaper said, that one could not get within fifty feet of him. Cervera then stood on the hotel veranda, bowing and shaking hands with members of the throng until manager William K. Hill ushered him indoors for a private reception. Hundreds watched the private event for two hours through the large-pane windows of the hotel dining room, cheering in response to the events inside illuminated by electric lights. Cervera, in clear English, toasted his captors, the city of Portsmouth, host Frank Jones, and manager Hill.

Cervera together with over a thousand prisoners departed Camp Long for the return trip to Spain in September as the tourist season closed. Thirty men who had died were buried on a knoll nearby and their bodies would not be retrieved until

ABOVE: *While hundreds of prisoners encamped for months in makeshift shelters, their leader hobnobbed among the wealthy Wentworth guests. Admiral Cervera, although in command of enemy forces during the Spanish-American War, was treated like a rock star during his Portsmouth visits. (PM)*

1916. Years later the much feared Portsmouth Naval Prison was built on the site of the encampment; though long abandoned, the castlelike structure stands there today. When five hundred American Marines arrived in Portsmouth the same summer, their officers were also wined and dined at the Wentworth, but the event barely captured a few paragraphs in the local paper.

Then came another burst of renovation. A series of increasingly elaborate brochures in the latter years of the Gay Nineties bear the names of Hill and Jones and show just how far the Wentworth grew. Elegant drawings and engravings show the hotel's new four-story wing, nearly doubling the length of the frontage to four hundred feet. The massive dining hall, now fitted with the revolutionary new plate-glass windows, which alternated with bay windows, faced the sea for a distance of 150 feet. One bay ran twenty-four feet wide, according to a full-page magazine advertisement, "so that not an iota of view is lost." A conservatory of rare tropical plants filled the north end. The new lobby, the heart of the hotel, now boasted octagonal plate-glass windows topped with a dome. From indoors, within sight of two cozy fireplaces, guests could now see Portsmouth and the intervening islands, as well as Kittery, the Navy Yard, and the very distant peaks of the White Mountains.

By night the outline of the hotel was illuminated by hundreds of small electric bulbs. From the sea, a Journal reporter suggested in 1895, "it must be the handsomest beacon that meets the eye of the mariner anywhere in his wanderings." The *Herald* in 1899 went even further. Viewing the hotel from Kittery, the writer said, "its grandeur dwarfs all other hotels on the Maine and New Hampshire coasts until they become almost insignificant."

Wentworth advertising spread the word. The evolution of the printed brochures during Hill's tenure demonstrate the rapidly advancing technology on the brink of the twentieth century. A later piece includes a full twenty-four pages of tiny, densely packed type on heavier glossy paper designed to highlight an amazing new addition—printed photographs. The sweeping panoramic shots of the view from the hotel are, however, disappointing to the modern eye. Like the popular "view books" of the era, the pictures appear flat and muddy, a wash of gray

ABOVE: *Portsmouth tycoon Frank Jones as an elder statesman. He died in 1902. (ATH)*

Office OF THE WENTWORTH

ABOVE: *Early hotel brochures sporting photographs were almost devoid of humans, as this page demonstrates. The figure of an African American boy on the stairway is a statue. The hotel remained "exclusive" until well into the mid-twentieth century. (ATH)*

without the sharp contrast of photos that would appear in print just a few years later. The images are almost entirely devoid of people, but to the Victorian eye, they demonstrated scientific proof that the broad claims of the Wentworth promoters were indeed true. Turning indoors, thankfully, Hill hired an artist to render the atmosphere of the new office and the dining hall, and these showed images of people. The elegant brochure was then stapled into a textured white cover complete with richly embossed lettering on a floral design of Oriental simplicity.

This 1890s promotion contains early examples of "name branding" and "co-marketing" that would become the fashion in hotel promotion. The final two pages of the booklet were effectively an ad-within-an-ad for the recently rebuilt Rockingham, also managed by Hill. The Wentworth was beginning to expand its calendar to what tourism people now call the "shoulder seasons" of spring and fall. Owning the Rockingham gave Jones a year-round destination. The invitational language in the ad oozed with a sense of exclusivity, as if the mere act of promotion was beneath the standards of the salesman:

> Hon Frank Jones, proprietor of the ROCKINGHAM, desires to set forth without exaggeration the advantages offered by the Rockingham as a model winter home. It is not said in any spirit of boasting that this has long been the verdict of the best informed travelers.

But the Victorian traveler also wanted accurate timetables and rate charts, all of which the Wentworth brochure provided. A full-page map shows train routes to Portsmouth from all over New England and from the Canadian Maritimes. Most prominent is a detailed chemical analysis of the water.

Visitors during the expanding Colonial Revival were equally interested in the science of the past. Brochures from the Hill era, influenced if not written by John Albee, still opened with a detailed history of New Castle, its political and military importance, and, of course, the lineage of the Wentworth family. The local fascination with Portsmouth-area history had reached national prominence largely through two editors of the prestigious *Atlantic Monthly*. William Dean Howells, who summered at Kittery Point, and held a special love for the region, as did his colleague, the poet and novelist Thomas Bailey Aldrich, whose hugely popular novel *The Story of a Bad Boy* (1869) chronicled his rambunctious Portsmouth childhood. During this era, extensive illustrated articles in such prestigious publications as *Harper's* focused on the local coastline. *Harper's* published sections of Aldrich's folksy new history of Portsmouth, *An Old Town by the Sea* (1895). The works of poets Celia Thaxter and John Greenleaf Whittier, both of whom died in the 1890s, still sold briskly even as their Romantic era teetered on the brink of extinction. The Wentworth, built not thirty years before, was becoming a grand "old" hotel.

ABOVE: *Frank Jones's monument to himself is still the tallest tomb in Portsmouth's South Cemetery. (JDR)*

This time Jones put his money into a new idea—a hotel within a hotel. The Wentworth "annex," built next to the huge recent addition, was designed to function independently. It had its own parlor and office, billiard area, rooms to sleep a hundred guests, and an innovative separate dining facility built onto the top floor. Visitors could now arrive in late June and stay until early September, a period that many residents of the New Hampshire seacoast find the most beautiful. The original tendency toward an "equality" of room design had by now given way to a wider range of quarters, from smaller short-stay rooms to extravagant apartments, suites, and separate cottages for parties of varying size and wealth.

The plan worked, at least initially. The next season opened with two hundred guests in residence, more than double the usual startup figure. Jones expanded his golf course, fully electrified the hotel from his private power plant, and ran his own water main from a private spring miles away. The State of New Hampshire helped out by constructing a new causeway with tax dollars, then debated funding a bridge to replace the one built twenty-five years earlier. A new mode of transport, the horseless carriage, was appearing with more frequency as the sport of "motoring" brought a new breed of traveling tourist. Politics won out, and the bridge was built using 75,000 feet of timber.

Although his political influence would linger on for years, Frank Jones would not. He had been secretly ill for years. Dying of Bright's disease, he kept his condition quiet for fear of panicking investors in his widely ranging companies. Jones's inner circle of trustees guarded the secret of his mortality. Only the sale of his brewery and then his racing stables at his mansion at Maplewood Farm in 1901 indicated the wholesale deconstruction of his empire soon to come.

Jones's last truly famous guest arrived quietly in August 1901. Admiral George Dewey, the hero of Manila Bay and the highest-ranking officer in the U.S. Navy, settled in for several weeks of rest at the Wentworth with his second wife, her maid and a Chinese valet. The second Mrs. Dewey was new to Portsmouth. She arrived wearing a black dress, veil, and black gloves, which pleased the *Herald*. The Admiral, though grayer

and defined by age, the paper noted, stood as straight as he had as a young man at the Navy Yard during the Civil War.

On hearing of the death of the Hon. Frank Jones on October 2, 1902, the town of Portsmouth grew silent, except for the peal of church bells, as businesses shut down. His body lay in state all the next day at the Middle Street Baptist Church as thousands of mourners passed by. Only the demise of George Washington or Abraham Lincoln affected the city more. Although he contributed little directly to the welfare of the community—he left no public buildings or major bequest—Frank Jones had rebuilt the fading town by the sea, commanding and receiving the respect of its growing population.

Like an ancient pharaoh, Jones had been preparing his own memorial. In 1880, the year after he purchased the Wentworth Hotel, Jones bought himself a large cemetery plot on the highest ground in Portsmouth's Harmony Grove, today part of the South Cemetery. There he had erected a monument to the Jones name sixteen feet high. Before he died, he replaced that with a granite spire towering twenty-nine feet above the graveyard. It is visible today from Little Harbor, just up a tree-lined road from the mansion of his royal predecessor, Governor Benning Wentworth, for whom the hotel is named. In death, as in life, Jones towered over all others. But he missed, by just three years, the towering event in the history of his favorite seaside hotel.

ABOVE: *With Jones's demise, the "golden" Victorian era ended for the Wentworth. Twentieth-century owners would recall the gay nineties with increasing nostalgia, all but forgetting the original owners of the hotel. (RMC)*

# Making History

O n July 22, 1905, Portsmouth Harbor exploded, liter-
ally. The largest dynamite charge ever set by human
hand to that date obliterated Henderson's Point,
within sight of New Castle village. Thousands of onlookers
gathered on the nearby shore to see if the carefully engineered
explosion would indeed blast away a troublesome spit of land
that had been a hazard to ships navigating the fast-flowing channel. Women with parasols and men in panama hats trained their
eyes on a ledge on the Maine side of the Piscataqua River, focus-
ing on the point locals called "Pull and Be Damned." Then the
world shuddered and the crowd gasped as a series of eruptions
sent plumes of earth (270,000 cubic yards of rock and soil) as
high as 170 feet above the river.

The Rockingham Hotel hosted a gaggle of reporters from
near and far to cover the doomsday explosion. Clusters of Wentworth Hotel guests traveled to the site in electric cars and were
among the three thousand cheering members of the crowd who
witnessed the thrilling exhibition of American ingenuity. Some
carried booklets published by the Frank Jones Brewing Company
that suggested the best vantage point for viewing the eruption
that took place near where the Spanish prisoners had encamped
seven years earlier. Despite rumors that the explosion might set
off a chain reaction that could destroy the planet, the bold solution worked. Forty thousand tons of rock and dirt were removed
in seconds. The only reported injuries of the day came when two

OPPOSITE: *In 1905, hordes of tourists
witnessed the massive controlled dynamite
explosion that obliterated a point of land that
had blocked navigation in Portsmouth
Harbor. (ATH)*

ABOVE: *Although distant news to New
Hampshire residents, media photographs
brought home the reality of the Russo-
Japanese War, which had claimed half a
million lives by 1905. (ATH)*

ABOVE: *President Theodore Roosevelt met with delegates of both Russia and Japan at his New York summer home prior to the Portsmouth peace negotiations that ended the Russo-Japanese War. This news service photograph and Roosevelt's later award of the Nobel Prize has led some to conclude incorrectly that he attended the treaty meetings. Left to right: Sergius Witte, Roman Rosen, Theodore Roosevelt, Jutaro Komura, Kogoro Takahira. (ATH)*

electric trolley cars, filled with people fleeing the region in fear, bumped into each other. But the great disappearing act at Henderson's Point was merely the warm-up for the show to follow—a show that would put the Wentworth Hotel in the global spotlight.

Half a world away from the seaside resort, Japanese and Russian soldiers were locked in an exhausting territorial war over Korea and the Sakhelin Islands. Astonishingly, half a million men had already died in the eighteen-month conflict. For Portsmouth residents, until the summer of 1905, it was a case of foreigners killing foreigners, an emperor battling a czar in a vague and mysterious land. Yet this war arrived like none before in history, and was depicted in modern newspapers as events occurred. Like unprecedented television coverage of the Vietnam War and Internet reporting in Iraq, correspondents with sophisticated new communication tools were turning war into a spectator event for millions. In the myriad of published combat photographs, it looks to contemporary eyes like a rehearsal for World War I. Men in endless rows crouch in trenches or creep forward, bayonets fixed. While the horrors of the two coming World Wars were not yet imagined in 1905, many feared that the Russo-Japanese War, the bloodiest war in world history to date, might spread into Europe and Asia as countries were forced to take sides and enter the fray.

Militarily, the island of Japan was showing remarkable skill against the massive Russian bear. Having taken on China in 1900 and having warned the Russian czar to stop his southern expansion toward Manchuria on the mainland, Japanese forces attacked Russian forces suddenly and successfully at Port Arthur on the Yellow Sea in neighboring Manchuria. When Russia responded by sending a fleet of sixteen modern destroyers and cruisers to retaliate, Japanese land artillery picked off all but one invading ship, suffering almost no losses of their own in the most successful military victory yet seen. But their heavy losses and costs had taken a toll on the island nation. Russia had the new Trans-Siberian Railroad line to replenish its army and a nearly limitless supply of peasant warriors, but the government, under the feeble hand of the last of the czars, was crumbling from within.

ABOVE: *Czar Nicholas II of Russia (top) and Emperor Mutsuhito of Japan. (ATH)*

Enter Teddy Roosevelt, the Rough Riding American president and media hero of the Spanish-American War. Despite his aggressive reputation as the first self-appointed global policeman, Theodore Roosevelt was also a skilled negotiator. Concerned that the balance of world power was shifting dangerously, he invited Japanese Emperor Mutsuhito and Russian Czar Nicholas II to lay down their swords and talk. A souvenir postcard of what would become known as the Treaty of Portsmouth shows the three men shaking hands, although they never actually met. Below their portrait is a quotation attributed to Roosevelt: "We are good fighters, but we want peace." All three world leaders stayed home as Japanese and Russian envoys arrived at what became a monthlong negotiation that ended with a cliff-hanger compromise. Both the Russian and Japanese delegations to the peace conference stayed at the Wentworth Hotel. When the event was over, Teddy Roosevelt became the first American president to win the Nobel Peace Prize and the estate of the late Hon. Frank Jones picked up the tab.

Exactly why Roosevelt selected little old Portsmouth remains a discussion point. Paris, The Hague, and Chefoo, China, were among the cities considered. Working hard to find the perfect conference site, the president wrote to the Japanese minister in Washington: "I am taking steps to try to choose some cool, comfortable and retired place for the meeting of the plenipotentiaries where conditions will be agreeable and where there will be as much freedom from interruption as possible."

Roosevelt knew the Piscataqua area was well defended. As former assistant secretary of the Navy, he had helped beef up the region's coastal defense system. Technically the treaty was negotiated at the Portsmouth Navy Yard, which is legally located in Kittery, Maine—a fact recently reconfirmed by the U.S. Supreme Court in a border battle between New Hampshire and Maine. America's oldest naval shipyard, established in 1800, celebrated its bicentennial in 2000.

Certainly Roosevelt, father of the Great White Fleet, knew the reputation of Portsmouth Navy Yard, home of the *U.S.S. Congress,* one of the original seven ships in the American navy and home to the *U.S.S. Kearsage,* which defeated the Confederate ship

OPPOSITE TOP: *Delegates traveled from New Castle to the Portsmouth Navy Yard in Kittery via steam launches. (ATH)*

OPPOSITE BOTTOM: *Delegates also traveled by auto and, as seen in this photograph from* Harper's Weekly, *by stagecoach. Here Japanese diplomats depart from the Wentworth for Kittery aboard the Tally-ho. (ATH)*

*Alabama* in the Civil War. He was likely aware that the Portsmouth shipbuilding tradition stretched as far back as 1690. He definitely knew that his boyhood hero John Paul Jones had launched the sloop-of-war Ranger from Portsmouth Harbor against the British in 1777. In fact, in 1905 Roosevelt's French emissary, Horace Porter, discovered the mummified 114-year-old remains of Captain John Paul Jones himself buried under the streets of Paris in a lead sarcophagus filled with alcohol. Earlier that same year Roosevelt had collected the corpse of the Scottish seaman and brought it "home" to America escorted by eleven battleships. Jones was reinterred in an elaborate crypt in the basement of the U.S. Naval Academy at Annapolis, Maryland, with great pomp.

More important, Roosevelt needed a welcoming town, a hospitable community that would not show favoritism or antagonism toward either the Russian or the Japanese envoy. Big cities might be distracting; the delegates needed time to hunker down together and talk. More-populated resorts like those at Bar Harbor, Maine, or Newport, Rhode Island, might have too many tourists, planners feared. Still, the meeting place had to be accessible, populated enough to host the envoys and the press and with enough scenic attractions to entertain the dignitaries when they were away from the negotiating table. New Hampshire Governor John McLane, a fishing and hunting buddy of Roosevelt, informed the administration that the Bretton Woods Hotel in the White Mountains and the Wentworth Hotel in New Castle were ready, willing, and available.

The first hint that the Wentworth had been chosen appeared in the Portsmouth paper in early July, exactly a month before the delegates arrived. Judge Calvin Page, the man most clearly in charge of Frank Jones's estate, offered to house and feed both delegations at no charge. As far as records show, although both delegations left a tip and a $10,000 payment to Goveror McLane, the Jones's estate was apparently not reimbursed, except in publicity, which is paying dividends to this day.

Locals considered hoping, even assuming, that Roosevelt would take charge personally. A week before the conference, a newspaper offered this bullish prediction:

JAPANESE RUSSIAN PEACE CONFERENCE

·BUILDING AT NAVY YARD USED AS CONFERENCE HALL·

PORTSMOUTH NEW HAMPSHIRE U.S.A 1905

·HOTEL WENTWORTH·QUARTERS OF THE ENVOYS AND THEIR SUITES·

ABOVE: *Souvenir postcards of the Treaty of Portsmouth featuring the Wentworth began to appear within two days of the meetings. This red, white, and blue card linked the hotel and the Peace Building at the Navy Yard as historic destination points. (LK)*

RIGHT: *Another popular postcard showed the Ambassador's Parlor in the Colonial Wing of the Wentworth. The Russians occupied this portion of the hotel, which has since been torn down. (ATH)*

The President will undoubtedly make his headquarters at The Wentworth while here and will, it's expected, give a banquet to the envoys and their companions. This would be the most important social event in the history of New Hampshire and would add to the fame of New Castle's splendid hostelry.

Some of the earliest newsreel footage ever shot in Portsmouth chronicles the arrival of the Russian and Japanese delegates. The New Hampshire National Guard and military bands marched through a town thronged with visitors and decked out in bunting. Boys and girls in their Sunday outfits ran beside the horse-drawn carriages as Jutaro Komura of Japan and Sergei Witte of Russia, each doffing his high top hat, gestured to the cheering crowds. The arrival by boat from the *U.S.S. Dolphin* and *U.S.S. Mayflower* was partially staged. Witte and his group had already arrived secretly by train and settled into the Wentworth. Both men had met privately with President Roosevelt at his summer home in Oyster Bay, New York, days earlier.

Wentworth employees narrowly avoided a political faux pas as the foreign envoys arrived. A hotel staffperson had raised the Japanese flag on the main tower of the hotel where it waved near the Stars and Stripes for half an hour. Meanwhile a porter, balancing the Russian flag on his shoulder, climbed to the tower of the hotel annex, but discovered no rope attached to the pole. The porter returned the Russian flag to the front office, and hotel employees went into a huddle. Without a sturdy rope to display the Russian banner, and with the envoys on their way to the Wentworth, employees quickly lowered the Japanese flag and sent their own envoy to the local hardware store to find a sturdy rope. Neither nation's flag was flying as the delegates entered the main lobby, but hours later with the new halyard in place, the Wentworth porters raised the opposing colors from the rooftops.

For one month the delegates shuttled back and forth by Navy cutter from the Wentworth to the secure brick "Peace Building" just across the Piscataqua River for the hard negotiations. A treaty room was hastily created in just four days, and a small memorial to that room survives today at the Portsmouth

Naval Yard. The world press, most of them housed at the Rockingham Hotel, reported every step of the process, formal and informal. The best and the brightest of the modern media sent constant dispatches, whether or not there was news. On a slow day, the fact that the delegates enjoyed New England brown bread and beans was telegraphed around the globe.

In one article a man and a woman wheeled their auto at high speed under the portico of the hotel annex, which housed the Russian delegation.

"I am Mr. Pingree of Boston," the man announced, leaping from the car. "I want to see Mr. Witte immediately."

"Mr. Witte is a busy man," said Mr. Korostovetz to Mr. Pingree. Witte's attendant had been quickly summoned. But "the man in 328" was busy. What was the nature, he asked, of Mr. Pingree's urgent visit?

"I lived in Russia for two years," Pingree explained. "I have experienced the hospitality Americans receive there and I want to shake Mr. Witte's hand and tell him I am obliged for my treatment."

Photographers immediately captured the extraordinary difference between the bearded Witte, more than six and a half feet tall, and the delicate frame of Komura, more than a foot and a half shorter. Cartoonists exaggerated the difference to the point where Komura appeared small enough to sit on Witte's knee. In American political cartoons, Roosevelt often appeared larger than both men. Witte and Komura were highly intelligent. Komura had attended Harvard while Witte spoke fluent French. Both were committed, even when their leaders were not, to ending the gruesome war and reaching a peaceful compromise.

The sticking point from beginning to end was the issue of remuneration. Having won battle after battle, the Japanese expected a cash indemnity for the cost of the war from the Russians. The Russians refused. Twice Witte was called home when Komura refused to back down on this point. Witte stayed, however, and in the final day of the negotiations, just when all appeared lost, Roosevelt asked Emperor Mutsuhito to withdraw his demand for indemnity. Komura was allowed to back down—a dishonoring act that made him wildly unpopular with the people of Japan—and the treaty was signed. On hearing the news, the mayor of Portsmouth ordered that church bells be rung for a full half hour, an expression of joy not seen in town since the end of the Civil War.

"Peace!" the *Portsmouth Herald* announced in five inch high letters on August 29, 1905. "Peace! That is the word that has electrified Portsmouth and sent a thrill throughout the world." The Treaty of Portsmouth was signed officially at the Navy Yard on September 5.

A century after the Russo-Japanese War, historians remain intrigued by just what went right in Portsmouth. The success of the treaty was by no means inevitable. Japanese political cartoons from the era picture the Russian bear devouring the globe while Russian soldiers gnaw on the bones of their victims. Anti-Asian illustrations depicted the Japanese as a subhuman race deserving of extermination. Yet something in the welcoming seacoast community mitigated all that for thirty crucial days. Something intangible spoke to Witte and Komura and to all the members of their delegations as they spent time among the locals, who urged them toward peace. A key factor in the creation of that hospitable environment was the Wentworth Hotel.

The technical term is multi-track diplomacy. While the diplomats hammered out the articles of peace in formal negotiations around the leather-covered walnut table at the Navy Yard, a flurry of social events influenced the foreign envoys away from the table. Witte complained in his diary that his rooms at the Wentworth were too small and the food at first not to his liking. When word of this hit the press, both Harvey and Wood, the Wentworth managers, and a Russian spokesman explained that reported complaints by Witte were "entirely false." Generally the delegates were thrilled with the lavish accommodations. Housed in separate wings of the hotel with private entrances, both delegations had similar accommodations, all with ocean views and private transcontinental communications. Some historians believe that Witte and Komura communicated directly during private walks through the hotel rose garden.

The delegates met informally at the hotel to work out details of the tentative peace. They posed for group photographs on the

ABOVE: *Political cartoonists made much ado about the comparatively short stature of the Japanese emperor and his diplomats. Japan, in the end, agreed to give up its demand for reparations, causing delegates to lose face in the final treaty outcome. (ATH)*

veranda and met at the hotel with Roosevelt's emissary. Although newspapers warned that the dignitaries would not be visible, both groups mingled openly with hotel guests. Witte, a master of public relations, seemed to revel in the attention; Komura was more private. Witte attended a piano recital at the hotel and was thronged by ladies from Portsmouth. Komura held a "Love Fest" ball at the hotel following the signing of the treaty. One newspaper account describes an impromptu performance on the hotel piazza by "three negro boys" singing "My Louisiana Lou" while other boys performed acrobatics on a bicycle, to the great delight of Russian delegates.

The Wentworth provided a safe, comfortable home base from which both Japanese and Russians could make day and evening trips. The teams moved in tandem, seemingly orchestrated actions as the diplomatic dance played out. After the Russians motored about the coastal roads in spiffy 1905 Pope-Toledo motorcars, the Japanese did the same. When the Russians attended church in Portsmouth, the Japanese went to church in Kittery. The Russians met with a Jewish group and the Japanese visited a Baha'i community in Eliot. After Komura visited New Hampshire politicians in Manchester, a group from the Amoskeag Mills there dined with Witte at the hotel. Both envoys gave identical contributions to York Hospital and the York Historical Society. Both visited the Isles of Shoals, traveled in the hotel's "Tally-Ho," attended the hotel theater and banquets, shopped in Portsmouth, and dined at the Wentworth with influential local figures.

Only the weather refused to cooperate. Not even the Wentworth, despite its scientifically proven records for cool weather and ocean breezes, could escape an oppressively hot and muggy summer. "M. Witte Expected It Would Be Cooler" the *Herald* announced on the front page on August 9. But the heat wave continued, bringing on an aggressive army of mosquitoes that plagued the peace process.

Ensconced safely in Oyster Bay, New York, Teddy Roosevelt monitored and manipulated the peace process. He arranged for a fancy garden party for Witte at Niles Cottage in New Castle. The Niles family had vacated for the month, allowing Assistant

Secretary of State H. O. Pierce and his family to host the Russians, then the Japanese. Roosevelt's emissaries raced back and forth from the Wentworth to Oyster Bay, among them his secretary William Loeb, father of the future controversial publisher of *The Manchester Union Leader*. The delegates were able to contact their leaders by transatlantic cable recently installed at Rye. From New York, Roosevelt cabled the czar and the emperor directly, finessing points of the treaty, and finally convincing the Japanese leader, for the good of all, to relent on his key demands.

The compromise ultimately pleased neither side. By backing down, the Japanese lost face, and Baron Komura suffered the anger of the Japanese people. Both nations, for a time, became American allies, then enemies, then allies again as the twentieth century unfolded. But the Treaty of Portsmouth is still seen by many as a textbook example of successful diplomacy. War was averted. Lives were saved. One of the world's first modern media events played out in an increasingly interconnected globe.

Wentworth staff members, at least, were satisfied with the peace conference. The Japanese delegation made good on promises to leave a generous tip. Mr. Witte and his assistant Baron Rosen matched the Japanese gifts, distributing one thousand dollars among hotel employees. Russian secretaries, according to the newspaper, tipped well too. A full accounting appeared in

ABOVE: *Japanese delegates motor up to the Wentworth among a host of visitors. Curious New Englanders turned out by the thousands to see and support the delegates during the treaty process. (ATH)*

print, and offers a look at the people behind the scenes who helped create the positive atmosphere in which the delegates operated.

The stewards and cooks were given $90 each; two girls who cared for the apartments of the plenipotentiaries received $30 each; ten French waiters were given $10 each; three table waiters, $30; fourteen bellboys, $10; two elevator boys, $31; two hat men $5.00 each; three porters, $40.00; mail carrier, $65.00. The private chef was also liberally rewarded. After that they called on the employees in other parts of the hotel who were not much in contact with the guests and left with them hundreds of dollars.

A final and little-known Treaty anecdote, a favorite of former *Portsmouth Herald* editor Ray Brighton, speaks volumes about the way the press covers world news. Besides transmitting more than two million words from the telegraph lines in Portsmouth, reporters had long gaps of time with little to amuse them. During the monthlong negotiations, the story goes, more and more reporters were seen wearing a distinctive badge made from a narrow strip of white satin knotted with a strip of yellow ribbon and bearing the initials OSVC. A number of Japanese delegates too sported the decoration and, at one point, so did Ambassador Witte, who was secretive about its origin during the conference.

The emblem turned out to be a prank. American reporters created the Society of the White Ribbon to parody the red ribbons worn by many European reporters. Fernando W. Hartford, owner of the *Herald,* was among the co-conspirators, mostly prominent journalists working for newspapers in Boston and New York. The acronym stood for "The Order of St. Vitus of Crete." The origin of the secret fraternity was later unmasked as an in-house joke. Long after the conference adjourned the *Herald* reported:

The society took its name from St. Vitus, who, like the modern newspaperman was continually jumping from place to place and the statement from an ancient Greek that "All Cretans

are liars." This statement was the grand password. The white of the society's emblem represented the innocence of the public; the yellow, the yellow streak in every newspaperman. The members were solemnly warned never to tell the truth if it could possibly be avoided.

ABOVE: *Since the signing of the treaty in 1905, international visitors have traveled to view Wentworth by the Sea, an increasingly important symbol of the successful peace process. Here, during the Smith ownership in the 1970s, Japanese visitors Fumihiko Togo, the Consul General, and his wife meet with Portsmouth City Councilman Bill Keefe. (ATH)*

# CHANGING PARTNERS

T he outsiders were coming. From time of the death of Frank Jones in 1902, the sale of the Wentworth Hotel had been inevitable. In his will, drafted by his friend and lawyer Calvin Page, Jones specifically mentioned the care of his two favorite hotels, the Rockingham and the Wentworth. They were to be maintained, he instructed his trustees, "in the same manner I would do if alive." To that end, Jones appointed William K. Hill, his longtime manager, among five powerful trustees. Hill's control, however, was limited to running the hotels. He was not included in the triumvirate of trustees, led by Page, who administered the vast holdings of the Jones empire.

Page quickly moved to fill Jones's shoes, stepping forward as spokesman for the tycoon's estate and slipping into a number of important corporate roles. The local press, still financially beholden to the Jones empire, accepted the affable heir apparent with enthusiasm. But even the Portsmouth Herald showed some subtle remorse when after eighteen years at the helm, William Hill suddenly resigned one season later. Historian Ray Brighton phrased it this way: "Whether Hill jumped or was pushed isn't known." His management style, so revered by Jones, apparently did not mesh with the goals of Calvin Page, Parker W. "Buck" Whittemore and Justin V. "Little Jesus" Hanscom, who collectively called the shots.

"Mr. Hill's departure will be generally regretted," the newspaper noted. "It was he who made The Hon. Frank Jones's name

OPPOSITE: *A ghostly woman reads in the parlor following the turn of the twentieth century. The painted cherubs and the ceiling dome are among the few interior features that have survived intact to this day. (ATH)*

ABOVE: *Calvin Page as a younger man in the 1880s. A lawyer and contemporary of Frank Jones, Page gained control of the tycoon's estate and negotiated the sale of the Wentworth along with Jones's other real estate holdings. (ATH)*

famous as a hotel proprietor." A number of key hotel staff resigned at the same time, perhaps as a gesture of solidarity, including the room clerk, the housekeeper, a steward, a wine clerk, and three chefs.

The replacement team, Harvey & Wood, had managed the Passaconnaway in York, Maine; the Bellevue in Boston; and other sites in Georgia and Florida and beyond. They immediately issued new ads and brochures indicating that the Rockingham and the Wentworth were in good hands, but Portsmouth hearts were still with the home team. It was a full year after his resignation, as the historic 1905 season dawned, before William K. Hill announced that he had accepted a prestigious post as manager of the Majestic, an eight-hundred-room hotel in New York. "No news more pleasing to the city in general has been received here in months," the *Herald* cooed.

As the Russo-Japanese War loomed, wealthy Wentworth patrons were absorbed with less weighty competitions on the golf links, on the tennis courts, in the swimming pool, and on the baseball diamond. Among the most debated topics, until the arrival of the foreign delegates, had been over the use of paid baseball "ringers," or "sandlotters," who filled in for absent players to boost a team's competitive edge. During the peace treaty negotiations, Russian Ambassador Witte caught one of these rough-and-tumble baseball matches at the Portsmouth Navy Yard field. In another Navy Yard game, a shortstop for the Wentworth Hotel crashed into the third baseman while chasing a fly ball. The injured man was taken to the hotel, where he was treated by the hotel's Dr. Hutchinson and a local physician. The following day the newspaper reported that the player was "still delirious" and needed a week to recuperate.

Apart from the peace treaty, managers Harvey & Wood had little in their three-year tenure to write home about. There was the annual visit of the Glidden Tour, in this case a parade of fifty automobiles whose owners made the sixty-three-mile trip from Boston on the first leg of their New England itinerary.

The Wentworth did host its first official "conferences" during this era, the new buzzword for short-term group bookings, the economic mainstay of commercial hotels in the

OPPOSITE TOP: *Although this photograph dates from the 1930s, it shows the familiar image of a band onstage at the Wentworth. Hundreds of performances have taken place here from the Victorian era to the present. (ATH)*

OPPOSITE BOTTOM: *The Wentworth lobby at the turn of the twentieth century, much as it appeared to treaty delegates and during the repeated sale of the hotel. (ATH)*

twentieth century. Groups from the DeMolay, the Oxford Club, Knights Templar, and religious organizations came to bask in the glory of the hotel that had hosted the famous treaty. Early conventions included the American Watch Company of Waltham, the Southern Shoe Wholesalers, the Bay State Automobile Association, seventy Boston assessors and their wives, and the Association of Edison Illuminating Companies.

By August 1906 rumors were flying that the Wentworth Hotel had been sold. Calvin Page adamantly denied it.

"We have not sold the Rockingham, nor leased the Wentworth," he told reporters. "At least I know nothing of such a deal and it is quite certain I would if it were consummated."

But the dismantling of the Jones empire was clearly under way. The Rockingham was, Page admitted, up for sale, and he hoped someone from Portsmouth would buy it. Jones's other resort hotel, the Sorrento in Maine, had been sold in 1904, and it burned to the ground in June 1906. By the end of the year, Harvey & Wood gave up operation of the two New Hampshire seacoast hotels. Who would manage them in 1907? The trustees said they did not know.

Then on April 27, 1907, the *Portsmouth Herald* announced the end of an era. The article appeared entirely in capital letters, although a number of details had to be repaired in follow-up stories. A New York brokerage firm, McDonald and Towle, had taken possession of both the Rockingham and the Wentworth. Frank C. Hall, of the Somerset in Boston, was named manager, but he in turn named two local managers whom he planned to oversee from Boston. The complex and lengthy deed filed in the Rockingham County registry at Exeter shows the property was actually transferred from the trustees of the Jones estate to a Mr. Stanley W. Tripp. Tripp soon transferred his ownership to a William H. White, from whom Loren D. Towle, of Newton, Massachusetts, eventually purchased the Wentworth, leaving Mr. W. J. McDonald holding the papers to the Rockingham. In a flurry of paperwork, the corporate Bostonians had arrived.

For the first time since 1879, the Rockingham and the Wentworth were under separate ownership, and they would not be joined again until two World Wars had passed. McDonald,

CHANGING PARTNERS   125

the Rockingham owner, immediately hired manager J. J. Butler to tear out the hotel billiard room and replace it with a new café. Butler placed a large ad in the Portsmouth paper with the headline: "Do you realize you have in your city the FINEST HOTEL IN NEW ENGLAND?" But something was rotten in the Rockingham, because when McDonald visited his renovated hotel in 1908, he immediately fired Butler and three weeks later sold the building.

The Wentworth fared no better. The newspapers offer only a glimpse of Loren Towle's single season as owner. His manager, Frank C. Hall, initiated the first motorboat races to the once stately hotel. Guests also participated in an automobile gymkhana. In the first event, participants ran a motorcar track at twelve miles per hour with the speedometer covered by a hood. The closest to the correct speed was the winner. In the second heat, traveling under eight miles per hour, contestants threw balls into five tubs lined up around the makeshift track.

In 1908 Towle sold the Wentworth to Albert H. Shaw, a timber dealer from Bangor, Maine, and Harry H. Priest, who managed a winter resort in Pinehurst, North Carolina. They created a corporation, the Wentworth Company, in the town of New Castle and issued stock.

Harry Priest often gets lumped in with the short-lived absentee Bostonian owners, lost in the shuffle between the golden years under Jones and the renaissance of the hotel as Wentworth by the Sea under the next owner, Harvey Beckwith, in the 1920s. But Priest appears to have been a solid manager in the tradition of Hilton and Hill, though without the ready cash of a robber-baron owner to call on. Instead of major changes, the Wentworth under Priest made the best of what it already had. The improvements, according to a sturdy twenty-four-page brochure, included hot and cold saltwater baths, well-equipped garages for motorists, long-distance telephones in every room, playgrounds for the little folks, new furnishing, and new "arrangements." Priest closed the fourth-floor dining area in the annex and replaced it with twenty new rooms, advertising luxury accommodations for a total of five hundred summer guests.

OPPOSITE TOP: *Advertising brochures sent to a largely urban clientele offered the scenic rural byways of New Castle as attractions. Roads initially perfect for strolling and carriage and horseback riding became equally popular for a new breed of early motorists. (ATH)*

OPPOSITE BOTTOM: *The Wentworth quickly became a key stopping spot for early automobile tourists. In this picture, antique car enthusiasts in the 1940s recall the golden days of the Glidden Tours, when scores of visitors arrived in motorcades traveling from Boston to Maine. (JDR)*

Newspaper coverage indicates that Priest kept the hotel busy and profitable for much of a decade as Americans shook off the formal nineteenth century and more and more families tested the freedoms of middle-class life and suffered the tragedy of World War. The public now favored active competitive sports of every kind over their parents' earlier search for history, scenery, and healthy air. Priest advertised the extensive athletic and recreational facilities at Hotel Wentworth as a "private park" managed by the Wentworth Company. Even the ancient island town became a sort of theme park, renamed Newcastle-by-the-Sea, adding the salty phrase that would later stick permanently to the hotel itself.

The strangeness of the times is evident in the opening paragraph of Priest's costly photo brochure. The text, groping and ungrammatical, seems drugged by a poetic ecstasy that the copywriter aches to describe, but cannot. The brochure begins:

> Yearning ever by nature of civilization's environment, for sunshine, pure air, blue skies—freedom—it is not strange that recollection of a visit to Hotel Wentworth lingers like a bright picture in memory's gallery. Fortune in location unsurpassed on the Atlantic Coast, with its vast Park and surrounding countryside ever and always backgrounded by the Sea in diversity of harbor and inlet, it at once becomes a spot set apart from all others and glorifies by the beauty of its environment; the Ideal so many have sought and so few have found.

Harry Priest's era is notable as much for what he did not accomplish as for what he did, and for moments of danger that flickered like a distant storm on the horizon. Even before his first summer season in 1909, Priest was campaigning for change. There was talk of bringing the trolley from Portsmouth around the loop at New Castle. Many town residents were in favor, as were the new Wentworth owners, but the outsider could not accomplish with his yeoman promotional efforts what the Hon. Frank Jones might have managed with a wave of his familiar hand. The Boston & Maine Railroad took a pass on the New Castle project. Taking another page from the Jones manual,

ABOVE: *With the later exception of Gloria Swanson, the best known Wentworth movie star was silent film actress Norma Talmadge who frequented the hotel in the Roaring Twenties. It is not known where this bathing beauty shot was taken. (JDR)*

OPPOSITE: *The problem of where to swim plagued hotel owners for the first half century. Under Harry Priest, the area behind the hotel continued to be the main swimming area, as it was under Frank Jones. The Little Harbor view (top) shows Leach Island, currently owned by the state of New Hampshire, in the distance. Bathers and boaters traveled down a long wooden stairway. (ATH)*

ABOVE: *Caught between two worlds, the
Wentworth in this era represented the best of
both the Victorian period and the modern
century of the motorcar. (ATH)*

Priest then campaigned to bring president-elect William Howard Taft to town. The Wentworth manager even sent photographs of attractive seaside homes to lure the chief executive, but to no avail. Taft eventually did stop by Portsmouth. There is a photograph of him standing outside the Rockingham Hotel in 1912, but the Wentworth did not rate a visit.

No news, even for a hotel, can sometimes be good news. In 1909 a front-page robbery at the hotel brought Priest north from his winter hotel in North Carolina. The Wentworth's winter caretaker, the son of the original manager, George E. Campbell, said a number of items had been stolen while the great white building was closed for the season. Police found a typewriter belonging to the hotel in the possession of a former soldier at old Fort Constitution, but no further news on the case was reported. In 1912 the hotel's icehouse, built in Frank Jones's time, burned at an estimated loss of three thousand dollars, although the ice was saved. In July 1913 visitors at the hotel watched in horror as an automobile crossing the bridge toward Rye crashed through the wooden railing and flipped twice in the air before sinking into the dark water. The driver, a well-known New Castle resident, was thrown from the car and plummeted headfirst against the rocks to his death.

But there was no recalling the dangerous automobile. Americans were in love with freedom at any cost and with motors at any price. In 1915 entrepreneur David Urch, who owned the New Castle toll bridge, decided to tackle the continuing problem of how to get hundreds of daily New Castle summer guests back and forth to Portsmouth. The jitney, a short-lived missing link between the horse cart and the bus, made its test run in May. Powered by a six-cylinder Studebaker engine, the jitney carried seven passengers, but could tow what the newspaper called "other smaller light motor-car basket trailers running either open or enclosed." Trailers held luggage or as many as six added passengers attached to the main car by a patent-pending connecting mechanism.

Although it ran for only a few years, according to at least one local historian the Urch jitney was the first of its kind in the nation, and the principle is still used to transport visitors in resort

ABOVE: *President Franklin D. Roosevelt reportedly told the local press in the 1930s that he had previously lodged at the Wentworth. Records of such a visit by the young assistant secretary of the navy have yet to be uncovered. During later visits to Little Harbor, Roosevelt stayed on his private yacht. (JDR)*

sites like St. Croix in the Virgin Islands. To assist the jitney up the steep incline at the entrance to New Castle at Cemetery Hill, Urch installed wooden planks at the far right of the dirt road to add traction. Planks on the bridges helped as well. The jitney route stopped in front of the Sinclair Inn, the brick mansion on Middle Street in Portsmouth originally built by Frank Jones for his daughter. It chugged through Portsmouth's South End, where boys playing in the street often hopped a free ride on the back car outside the driver's view. It stopped again at New Castle village at a shelter near the church called "The Wait-a-While," then circled up around the Hotel Wentworth and back.

Marion Hett Wendell, who ran the Wentworth gift shop during the Smith era, recalled the famous Urch family toll bridge during a 1974 interview in the weekly seacoast newspaper *Publick Occurrences.* Born in 1889, Hett accompanied her father as he delivered guests and their steamer trunks from Portsmouth to the Wentworth. She recalled walking fearfully over the drawbridge as her father's horse and carriage followed. David Urch was famous she said, for his "circus type" entertainment at the bridge. He kept an aquarium in a building near the tollhouse and featured trained horses that would leap from the second floor of the aquarium into the river to the delight of tourists.

As a child, Hett accompanied her father to visit the famous Spanish prisoners when he delivered milk. She remembered the prisoners trading their brass buttons to locals as souvenirs for cigarettes. In 1908, during Harvey & Wood's brief management era, Hett entered a rigorous local swimming contest, racing two ocean miles from Wallis Sands in Rye to Odiorne Point near the Wentworth. Standard swimming attire for women then consisted of a one-piece black mohair suit with a sailor collar stitched in white braid, a mohair skirt buttoned at the waist, silk stockings, bathing shoes, and a hat. Despite the heavy outfit, Hett bested all others, male and female, to capture the trophy.

Competitive rifle shooting, too, became an acceptable sport for wealthy female guests. Harry Priest introduced Annie Oakley to Wentworth patrons. The former girl star of Buffalo Bill's Wild West Show had grown rich and famous and settled down in the resort town of Pinehurst, North Carolina, with her

ABOVE: *The hotel's most famous employee, a mature Annie Oakley, taught society women rifle shooting. (LIB)*

OPPOSITE TOP: *The New Castle toll bridge was owned by the Urch family. This stopping point became a destination unto itself with an aquarium, tourist information, and a high-jumping horse that plummeted into the water. (BD)*

OPPOSITE BOTTOM: *For a brief period, toll bridge owner David Urch transported hotel guests in a motorized jitney that stopped at the popular "Wait-A-While" in New Castle village. (ATH)*

husband, William Butler. But America's most famous marksman missed the spotlight. It was probably not difficult for Harry Priest, who also managed the fashionable Carolina Hotel in Pinehurst, to convince "Little Sure Shot" to demonstrate her skills to an appreciative New Hampshire audience. While war ravaged Europe in 1916, the famous American gunslinger, then fifty-six years old, exhibited her horsemanship and shooting skills for the benefit of the Red Cross at the Wentworth.

Oakley, best known today as the source of the successful Broadway play *Annie Get Your Gun*, officiated at the horse-and-gun show that followed. The painter Edmond C. Tarbell, of New Castle, also a top-notch golfer, won the riding event. Mrs. Edward Horn, of New York, won the rifle contest, scoring 121 out of 150 targets at the hotel's "shooting grounds," probably on the grounds of the Wentworth Country Club today. Mrs. Horn's daughter, now in her nineties and living in New York, remembers the contest to this day. The winner, she says, received a "golden gun" trophy presented by Annie Oakley herself.

The great Victorian seaside hotels and their managers were fading fast. In 1914, while guests and staff watched from the grounds, the famous Appledore Hotel at the Isles of Shoals burned.

The Wentworth, still vital and ready to adapt, was barely approaching middle age when the next regime changed. In 1917, after forty-five years of managing grand hotels like the Wentworth, Harry Priest retired. He had arrived in 1908, the year the original Wentworth manager Charles Campbell died. The year before Priest left, former Frank Jones manager William K. Hill died at his Middle Street home in Portsmouth.

The past, that commodity so important to patrons of the Wentworth, was vanishing. The future, too, was as indistinct as a sudden fog. Ships filled with young American men and women were disappearing on the horizon, steaming across the Atlantic and into a distant war.

ABOVE: *Sarah Campbell (top) and Charles E. Campbell in their elder years. The original owners of the Wentworth Hotel continued to operate their guest cottage nearby for decades. Charles died in 1908. (CAM)*

OPPOSITE: *The adopted son of Charles and Sarah Campbell continued to work as a Wentworth caretaker well into the twentieth century. Here Henry Campbell poses in the driver's seat of one of the hotel carriages. (CAM)*

# From War to War

The retirement of partner and manager Harry Priest forced Wentworth co-owner Albert Shaw to draft another of his top men into service in New Hampshire. Shaw ordered Charles A. Judkins, a veteran hotel manager at the isolated Mt. Kineo House in Moosehead, Maine, to report on the double to the posh New Castle resort.

With American youths dying in The Great War overseas, by 1918, the hospitality industry was under intense federal scrutiny. It was a dangerous time for hoteliers. Under President Woodrow Wilson, hotels could be seized by the government and used as dormitories for workers turning out products for the war effort. The Passaconnaway, already closed to visitors, became part of this enforced program, and in February, Judkins walked the frigid grounds of the Wentworth with a federal agent, who surveyed the hotel to consider impressing it, too, into military service.

Portsmouth, with its famous Navy Yard, always busy in times of war, especially felt the population pinch. The federal and private shipyards were at full capacity. In 1877, when the Wentworth was new, as few as seventy-one civilian shipyard employees worked at the Navy Yard nearby. From 1917 to 1919, the number rose to more than five thousand workers, three times the peak during the Civil War. In fact, the nation's first government-subsidized housing development, Atlantic Heights, was established at Portsmouth in 1918. Designed in just ten

OPPOSITE: *An action view of young, wealthy Wentworth by the Sea guests sailing into the rocky 1930s. (ATH)*

days, completed less than eight months later, the million-dollar project included 150 brick dwellings for 278 worker families at the Atlantic Corporation's nearby shipyard. When workers at the local yards celebrated their success in hitting production quotas for the war effort, they did so at the Wentworth Hotel.

In March, Judkins and other hotel and restaurant managers went to Washington, D.C., to learn about new regulations on supplies to hotels, especially the scarcity of wheat. German U-boats were creating havoc with shipping, and Americans finally felt a twinge of the shortfall Europeans had been suffering for years. Meanwhile, regulations on liquor, a harbinger of Prohibition, threatened one of the fundamental profitmakers in the hotel industry.

Having ducked dormitory duty and with its budget trimmed, the Hotel Wentworth opened on schedule in June 1918. The Champernowne Hotel on Gerrish Island in Maine was not so lucky. Although its owners, too, had advertised and begun booking for summer, the hotel was taken over by the federal government just as the season was about to open.

Wentworth guests added the thrilling new sport of submarine sighting to their summer activity list. The Navy Yard produced its first two Portsmouth-built subs in 1917 and 1918 and would launch thirty-one more before the next war. During World War II, from 1941 to 1945, another eighty-one vessels were produced in record time at Portsmouth Yard. Initial testing of early submarines, as well as repair and refueling visits by other subs, took the craft up and down the black underwater Piscataqua highway, past New Castle, and into the Atlantic and around the Isles of Shoals. Guests with binoculars scanned the waves for the dark hulls that would sometimes breach at night so that submariners could get their bearings against the bright electric lights of the great white hotel.

Journalist Walter Cronkite refers to such a scene during World War II in his book *North by Northeast*. Cronkite recalls, "Visible from miles at sea . . . is the seemingly endless expanse of one of the country's finest old Victorian hotels, Wentworth by the Sea."

With its new thirty-by-twenty-foot American flag waving, the mammoth Wentworth hotel was also a perfect target for

OPPOSITE TOP: *The Naval Prison at Portsmouth was and remains an imposing structure, still visible from the hotel. (BD)*

OPPOSITE BOTTOM: *Submarine spotting became a new pastime for hotel visitors. Portsmouth produced a large number of subs during the first and second world wars. (ATH)*

marauding enemy subs and ships checking out the shipyards and military bases nearby. But even after the sinking of the *Lusitania*, the enemy had never been considered a real threat to American shores. The United States was still invincible. In 1941, that view would be shattered and Harry Beckwith would be forced to close the mighty Wentworth for the first time.

But not so during the first World War. Besides submarines, patriotic hotel guests were also fascinated by the new Navy prison, completed in 1912, that loomed like a concrete castle on the same spit of land where the Spanish prisoners had encamped. A Wentworth brochure from this era lists the prison, along with the New Castle tollbooth and military bases among the top "historic" island sights. Borrowing the name once reserved for the original Great Island fort, shipyard workers referred to the prison simply as the Castle. Expanded first to hold just over three hundred inmates, this New England Alcatraz would reach a capacity of three thousand men and become an institution feared by military seamen. Until the early 1970s, as portrayed in the film *The Last Detail*, just the word *Portsmouth* was synonymous with harsh prison life. In the early twentieth century, few seaside buildings except the Wentworth matched its monumental size. It survives today, crumbling in disuse, like an evil twin, a sort of anti-hotel where life was hell on earth for thousands of involuntary guests.

Despite the buildup of military camps just down the road, the Wentworth stayed open and active right through World War I, though with decidedly more flag waving and fewer luxuries than usual. The 1919 season following the armistice and peace was a boom year for New England hotels. Wealthy Americans who would have preferred to vacation abroad decided to stay closer to home—and party. Annie Oakley was back with her popular shooting school. Military bands played, couples danced in the moonlight, and the Wentworth was brimful of guests and conferees.

Buy low, the real estate mantra goes, and sell high. Just as the Jones's trustees had taken advantage of the hotel's fame after the Treaty of Portsmouth, owners Harry Priest and Albert Shaw now saw an opportunity to cash in on their New Hampshire

ABOVE: *Manufacturer Harry Beckwith also owned the nearby Farragut Hotel in Rye. He officially changed the hotel name to Wentworth by the Sea. (RMC)*

OPPOSITE TOP: *Well-dressed guests line up for putting practice outside the hotel. (ATH)*

OPPOSITE BOTTOM: *Famed course designer Donald Ross reshaped the Wentworth golf links during the 1930s. (ATH)*

investment—but quietly. In November 1919, just a year after Armistice Day, and as the hotel began its hibernation, Priest and Shaw sold the Wentworth to a corporation from Massachusetts. The hotel's next twenty-seven years are closely associated with the new director, Harry H. Beckwith, of Brookline, but like that of Frank Jones, Beckwith's presence emerged slowly. The Wentworth Company, now owned by Beckwith and with company president Archie E. Hurlburt of Boston, was officially in the hands of manager John P. Tilton.

Announcement of the sale—FAMOUS HOTEL CHANGES HANDS—barely caused a ripple in the local press; residents were now used to the comings and goings of corporate hotel men. More appealing was Harry Beckwith's pledge to immediately begin renovating the Victorian building. Renovation meant local jobs, and manager Tilton often kept a small crew of painters and carpenters busy off-season. Again like Frank Jones, owner Beckwith kept his word and opened his wallet, expanding the hotel until it enveloped the western end of the island, just a mile from the sleepy colonial village. Where Shaw and Priest had kept the Wentworth big and busy, Beckwith enlivened it with new purpose. Mirroring the postwar economy, Beckwith and company began vigorously in the 1920s, then nearly stalled in the Depression, revived in the latter thirties, and finally tumbled back into war.

A manufacturer by trade, Harry Beckwith was in the hotel game for the fun of it, and likely for the tax advantages. Beckwith's family made the successful hundred-year evolution from felt products, to shoes, to plastics. Among his companies, he owned the Beckwith Box Toe Company in nearby Dover with his brother Fred. He also owned the Studebaker House and the

ABOVE: *The dolphin theme established by New Castle tavern owner Sam Wentworth in the 1600s was given an art deco twist in the thirties under Beckwith. (ATH)*

Farragut Hotel, both in Rye. The hotels were his "playthings," according to a descendant, a place to impress his Boston friends and business colleagues.

Some of the credit for Beckwith's success with Wentworth by the Sea must go to manager Frank Tilton, an energetic man in his thirties. Tilton had a winning way with both employees and guests. The promised renovation began small—twenty-five new baths added to the 225 already available, improvements to the popular golf course, a new bowling alley, and the usual painting and refurbishing. Always renovating, Tilton increased the number of rooms by cutting down larger suites and adding windows. Beckwith modernized the old Victorian porch and added rooms to the Colonial annex, where the porch had been. Seaplane rides and water skiing behind motorboats were added to the list of activities with a calculated emphasis on fun for the

ABOVE: *"The Ship" appeared in the Beckwith era surrounded by a complex saltwater pool that had to be refreshed every few days. The structure, including its own theater, was razed in recent years to make way for new hotel accommodations. (ATH)*

young. Two sports—golfing and swimming—sum up the Beckwith-Tilton enhancements. In each case he hired the best and spared no expense.

According to golf historian Michael Hassel Shearer, the first Wentworth course had been designed by Alex H. Findlay, a recent émigré from Scotland, under Frank Jones in 1899. Findlay's work had put the Wentworth on the elite golfer's map. Two decades later, Beckwith quickly brought in Donald Ross, still remembered as one of the best golf course designers of all time. The owner had apparently met Ross at Pinehurst through former manager Harry Priest. Beckwith purchased an added parcel of land to give Ross more space to rebuild what players still remember as one of the finest nine-hole courses in New England. According to one newspaper account, Ross built two original holes and improved the rest of the course. His work survived with little further adaptation from 1921 until 1964, when the Smiths altered and expanded the Wentworth links to accommodate eighteen holes.

Harry Beckwith himself was an avid golfer. He put up special prizes that attracted the cream of the crop to compete at the scenic, Scottish-style course laid out along some of the most beautiful property on the New Hampshire coast. Early on, the new owners ruffled local feathers when, for two years following the war, manager Tilton allowed Boy Scouts from distant regions to tent on the hotel grounds. The Scouts doubled as an army of golf caddies and, as one elderly Portsmouth resident remembers, nearly caused a war with boys from the city's South End, who had traditionally caddied at the Wentworth.

The most visible Beckwith change was the Ship, a massive new wooden building shaped like a cruise boat and located between the hotel pier and the bridge to Rye. A less-than-impressed critic in the *Hartford Courant* half a century later would refer to it as "an ocean liner stuck on a reef."

Without a good beach to compete against nearby New Hampshire and Maine resorts, the Wentworth had to continually reinvent its swimming facilities to suit modern visitors. A little sandy area with bathhouses by the pier sufficed initially for waders and hardy athletes able to handle the icy Atlantic. Since

OPPOSITE TOP: *For three decades "The Ship" pool created an artificial "beach" much superior to the Little Harbor area at the back of the hotel. Guests were able to swim to the strains of a live orchestra imported from Boston. (ATH)*

OPPOSITE BOTTOM: *Powerful motorboats launched the new sport of waterskiing, although here on aquaplanes. The image of a youthful clientele was part of the hotel's marketing plan, although elderly summer patrons still dominated the guest list. (ATH)*

the time of Frank Jones, the safest swimming spot was at the back of the Little Harbor side of the hotel, where a man-made dam turned the inlet into a private salty lake.

Beckwith went one step further. Relying on the latest technology, his engineers created a deep ocean-fed pool with a cement floor. The pool opened in 1922 and kicked off a new Wentworth tradition, the Water Carnival, which initially attracted three hundred spectators. But maintaining the giant tank was no easy task. Ruth Kitching, who managed the pool into the Smith era with her husband, Norm, explained that the massive fifty-yard oval tank had to be pumped out and cleaned at low tide every three days. If low tide arrived at four in the morning, that's when the cleaning crew scrubbed the twelve-foot walls. Then the nine-foot tide refilled the cement pool with fifty-degree ocean water that had to be warmed using an elaborate heating plant installed in the Ship.

"We could run that boiler from one weekend to the next," Kitchiner told *Publick Occurrences*. "We would barely get the water to sixty-two degrees when the pool needed cleaning again."

Beckwith launched his Ship Casino overlooking the new pool. An ensemble of Boston Symphony musicians, in the years before Tanglewood, played as visitors took tea on the double decks of the Ship. Inside the building, guests viewed live theater productions, watched films, and even attended boxing matches. During recreational periods, to help swimmers coordinate their movements, the hotel dance band played up-tempo tunes.

The most distinctive sound of the Roaring Twenties was a chorus of female voices. Women by the hundreds had worked in the shipyards during the war. Now women had the vote. Women bobbed their hair, showed their ankles, smoked cigarettes, created art, drove motorcars, flew airplanes, and moved boldly into every traditional male role that was not locked and bolted.

The dramatic change is evident in the way Portsmouth celebrated its founding. In 1823 a select group of upstanding white male citizens had paraded somberly through the streets, then attended a male-dominated church service, where they took turns offering lengthy formal speeches honoring the great heroes of Portsmouth's first two hundred years. Then they joined their women for a formal dance. The tercentennial bash in 1923, by contrast, was a coed affair in which hundreds of gaily costumed figures acted out great tales of local seacoast history, complete with horses, stagecoaches, muskets, fishing boats, and both friendly and renegade Indians. The Indians, bare chests sweating in a feverish, even erotic performance, were hired professional ballet dancers imported from Washington and New York City. Women in flowing Greco-Roman gowns stood in classical poses representing each of the towns in the seacoast region and each of the godly virtues of humankind. The pageant was orchestrated by Virginia Tanner, a New Castle summer visitor. Tanner not only convinced the town fathers to let her stage the celebration, but received a budget of $12,000 as well.

Amid a sea of popular male golfers who walked the improved Wentworth course, champion Glenna Collett stands out. Known as the Queen of Amateur Golf, she played for the love of the sport, collecting only the occasional prizes put up by owners like Harry Beckwith. A natural athlete, Collett had taken first to baseball, then tennis, and finally to golf, and even quit high school to play. She had already won the U.S. amateur women's title when she competed on the new Donald Ross course at the Wentworth in the early 1920s. Collett went on to win five more American titles and played until she was in her eighties.

In 1925 manager Tilton hired swimming champion Helen Wainwright, "the world's greatest mermaid," to oversee programs at the new Wentworth pool. For three months' summer work she was reportedly paid five thousand dollars in an era when one summer waitress remembers earning $150 all season. Wainwright taught "embryo" swimming and diving classes and offered exclusive exhibitions as hotel spectators watched from the decks of the Ship, then ducked inside for drinks and a round of bridge. Although she could not compete with amateurs, Wainwright arranged a fantastically successful two-day Water Carnival that drew a host of amateur Olympic swimmers and thousands of spectators from every town and resort in the region.

ABOVE: *New Castle summer resident Virginia Tanner orchestrated the elaborate Pageant of Portsmouth celebration for the region's tercentennial in 1923. (ATH)*

ABOVE: *Olympic champion Helen Wainwright signed a contract to give swimming lessons and present diving exhibitions at the Wentworth for a summer salary of $5,000. (LIB)*

No resort on the East Coast, according to a slick oversized photo brochure, could compete with the extraordinary tennis, boating, golf, and swimming facilities at the newly renamed Wentworth by the Sea. Under Beckwith, for the first time, the full grandeur of the hotel could be captured in print and, thanks to aerial photography, the sheer size of the campus was revealed. These two dozen images from the early thirties are the clearest pictures we have of the Wentworth in action. Not only are they the most detailed, but for the first time the photographs also include people—not just distant blurry figures caught accidentally on film, but full-scale humans.

In the Beckwith booklet, for the first time too, we see youths. Five teenagers standing on large flat wooden sleds water-ski behind a motorboat. A couple in matching striped coats lean back dramatically, balancing their fast-moving little sailboat. Two girls in white ankle socks, legs crossed, sit reading in a corner of the piazza. A woman in a fur wrap and bonnet holding a golf club waits for a turn on the crowded putting green near the tennis courts. Bathers lounge under shade umbrellas or wiggle their toes in the saltwater pool outside the Ship. Both the six-man dance band and the twelve-member symphony orchestra pose in formal attire.

Not a single elderly face is featured in the lavish Beckwith-Tilton brochure. By contrast, former employee Frank H. Stanton remembers a sea of older faces; there was an equal mixture of guests aged fifty to eighty, he recalls. Many had spent all ten summer weeks at the Wentworth for a generation or more and held territorial claim to specific chairs in the parlor and on the piazza.

Each photograph is a time capsule too, displaying the latest furnishings and decorations but offering glimpses of architecture spanning a half century. The booklet includes full-page studies of the lounge; the rotunda in the lobby, which still survives; the great dining hall; the green room; the old ballroom; and the new card room. We get a detailed view of a typical guest room, a survey of the sculptures in the parlor imported by Beckwith from his trips to Italy, a close-up of the Wentworth Golf Club, and a detailed aerial map of Donald Ross's nine-hole course. Beckwith incorporated the new panoramic technology as well, and the inside page folds out to the familiar view from the front of the hotel—a photograph nearly three feet wide.

Gone too is the fumbling amateur prose from the Harry Priest era at the dawn of the twentieth century. Now the writing is confident, professional, and brief. With a nod to the nearby mansion of Royal Governor Benning Wentworth, the brochure opens with two lines from Longfellow's poem *Lady Wentworth:*

"Where his great house stood looking out to sea
A goodly place where it was good to be."

The Colonial Revival in the Piscataqua, begun in the 1860s, had faded away by 1930. History, other than this brief reference, is as absent from Beckwith and Tilton's promotional copy as elderly patrons are from the photos. For those who prefer to rest, rather than to recreate, the copywriter notes, there are plenty of airy nooks and crannies to be found. The brochure mentions a new artesian well for healthy drinking water and the installation of three thousand sprinklers. But overall, the emphasis in the Jazz Age was on being alive and lively, with the past seen more as a quaint and curious backdrop rather than something to be studied and revered.

Even as a wave of youthful visitors from across the nation discovered the new and improved Wentworth by the Sea, two age-old traditions refused to die. The guests remained white Christians and the help remained servile. No written rules barred guests of color. None was needed in a nation where racism was still sewn into the fabric of society. President Wilson, raised in a Southern Presbyterian family, was clearly not on the side of civil rights, and during his administration segregation became the law of the land.

Harry Beckwith took discrimination a step further by promising his guests by private letter that they would receive the finest in Gentile accommodations. Western Union telegrams in the Portsmouth Athenaeum archives reveal private cables from the Wentworth Company to a bank and another hotel inquiring about the "nationality" of potential summer guests. A telegram

ABOVE: *Owner Harry Beckwith and family wander the hotel grounds. This photograph was included in a trade magazine for shoe manufacturers. (RMC)*

from the Foster Travel Service in response reads: "Mrs. Hart is Hebrew prominent socially a charming woman." Another report from Mr. Foster assures the hotel that the guest is a "good American through and through." A direct descendant of Harry Beckwith argues that he did have Jewish friends but preferred to pay their way at the Wentworth rather than officially record their names in the register.

Wealthy visitors, once they were vetted by the hotel, were treated like royalty. The hotel staff was strictly trained to exhibit "the highest standards" while maintaining the lowest profile possible. Outside fraternization between the help and visitors was verboten. This attitude, Harry Beckwith promised in his lush 1930s brochure, prevailed in the beauty parlor, buffet, garage, valet, and laundry. He guaranteed "friendly and sincere" efforts from the management and "quiet, intelligent and self-effacing service from all employees." In the single brochure photo that includes staff members, two young women serving five o'clock tea stand demurely, heads bowed, eyes averted from the camera.

Former employee Frank Stanton remembers a less-than-perfect operation. The old steam elevator was quite dangerous. Stanton moved the elevator up by pulling on a long handle that passed through a two-foot-long slot in the floor. Pushing the handle forward moved the elevator down. The "neutral" area in the center was affected by the momentary surge of steam power, so it was not always possible to stop directly level with the floor while guests entered and left. Stanton remembers two elderly sisters shrieking in fear as he stepped from the elevator to let them in—and it began to rise.

Despite the range of activities, Stanton says, most older guests didn't do much. At sixteen dollars per day, they lived from one elaborate multicourse Wentworth meal to the next, receiving service in direct proportion to the generosity of their tips. Mayor Curley of Boston often visited with his "henchmen" and tipped a dollar simply for bringing a bucket of ice. Room clerks, Stanton recalls, got a small salary plus commission on extra items billed to guests—cigars, newspapers, baths. One clerk made a habit of breaking wind loudly while at the same time speaking politely to departing guests with the lowest room bills.

Stanton was on hand in 1936 when Jerry Gray, leader of the seven-piece hotel dance band, explained to Wentworth manager Richardson that he had gotten a better offer from another band and wished to break his summer contract. Gray went off to join the famed Glenn Miller Band and orchestrated "Begin the Beguine" and dozens of other hit songs for Miller. "I'm damned glad to get rid of him," was all the manager had to say. "One less to pay."

Stanley B. Lacks vividly remembers the life of a hotel family. His parents, who met at the Wentworth and married in 1911, were among a core of staff members who migrated with the seasons from New Castle to the Carolina in Pinehurst, North Carolina. His father made the trip for thirty-seven years. Lacks stayed with his mother for a time at the Campbell Cottage and grew up at both resorts, eventually working as a doorman. Workers tended to keep positions at both locations and were part of an extended family—bellboys, pages, waiters, doormen, parlor maids, housemen, porters, cooks, hairdressers, waitresses—all working seven days a week.

Lacks remembers Captain Nye, who ran the cruise ship from the Wentworth dock in the Beckwith era and wintered as the night watchman at the Carolina. Then there was Frieda Marks, who checked women's fur coats at both hotels as guests came to dinner. Her job, distinct from the hatcheck woman, was so important that her income, after tips, rivaled that of the head-waiter. In an extensive oral history, Lacks describes life in the staff dorms, the hardship of moving with the seasons, and details about employee uniforms, luggage, romance, and pay.

Though Gatsby was in vogue elsewhere, the ultimate Wentworth hotel chic was still the annual masquerade ball. Employees too got a taste. Each summer season now concluded with a staff masquerade the day following the guests' affair. No longer locked into Wentworth dormitories at night, as they were in the W. K. Hill era, workers under John Tilton nearly a half century later still accepted their subservient status as part of the professionalism of their industry, in which no protective unions existed. The "pros" were career staff who migrated with the seasons, and saw themselves as a cut above the locals, who worked largely for

tips during high school and college vacations. This young under-class inevitably got the worst tasks and the lowest tips.

Tilton managed to hold these disparate worlds together, even in crisis. In December 1922 the *Herald* reported a suspicious fire at the Wentworth. Tilton himself had been the first to spot the blaze in the crawl space under a wing of the hotel. The fire sent up billows of black smoke after igniting layers of oakum smeared on the steam pipes. Tilton and a large group of men renovating the off-season hotel kept the blaze under control until the Portsmouth Fire Department arrived. The following year a summer guest reported two thousand dollars in jewelry stolen from her room. A hotel employee was arrested, but was released for lack of evidence. And in 1926 a sudden summer gale blew down the chimney at the hotel powerhouse, nearly killing the resident fireman.

But the greatest disaster of Tilton's tenure was his own demise. In July 1927, while traveling to oversee a number of Harry Beckwith's investments, Tilton died suddenly aboard a train returning from North Carolina. The energetic, imaginative Wentworth manager was just forty-two, taken down at the same age as his predecessor Frank Hilton. The *Herald* under F. W. Hartford, editor and friend of the late Frank Jones, offered an effusive eulogy for another fallen manager of the region's famous hotel.

Had Arthur E. Richardson, Beckwith's next manager, been able to predict the future, he might have thought twice about taking over the Wentworth helm. Manager Tilton had weathered a small fire, petty theft, and blustery winds on his watch. But Richardson's course would run him smack into Black Thursday, Prohibition, and the Great Depression. And amazingly, he took the Wentworth through unscathed, only to run his mighty ship aground on the shores of World War II.

Yet, invigorated by a new mobile America, the late 1920s and early 1930s were far from doom and gloom at New Hampshire's premier seaside resort. The old toll bridge at the village end of New Castle had been replaced after 104 years by a modern bridge at the expense of New Hampshire taxpayers. Road crews also renovated the bridge on the Wentworth side to accommodate the flow of motorcars, now essential to modern

American life. That summer, winners of the annual costume ball hailed from such faraway cities as Canton, Ohio; Orange, New Jersey; and Louisville, Kentucky; as well as Boston, Chicago, New York, and Philadelphia. Conventions were at an all-time high as lawyers, bankers, pharmacists, telephone stockholders, jewelers, newspaper owners, Rotarians, chambers of commerce, and accountants, naval, governmental, fraternal, and charitable groups booked their annual events. Harry Beckwith, now the sole owner of the Wentworth, increased his hands-on role, expanding the hotel structure, constantly improving the floral grounds, enhancing his beloved golf course and the Ship, which now offered "talkie" films.

As Ray Brighton noted, no bankrupt stock market investor jumped from the roof of the hotel following the infamous Wall Street Crash in October 1929, perhaps because the stock market plummeted just after the close of the tourist season. If anything, that year is most notable for a small gathering of the nation's governors, a predecessor to the full-blown Governors' Convention held at the Wentworth in 1948. The group met in New London, Connecticut, and planned to travel to Bretton Woods in the New Hampshire mountains to witness the dedication of *Old Peppersass,* the original Mount Washington engine of the popular Cog Railway.

That gave Fernando W. Hartford, owner of the *Portsmouth Herald* and the *New Hampshire Gazette,* an idea. A tireless promoter of Portsmouth, and seven times mayor of the "city of the open door," Hartford had learned his politics at Frank Jones's knee. Jones had loaned Hartford the money to buy the *Penny Post* and convert it into the *Herald.* In the intervening years, Hartford had methodically purchased every other newspaper in the city—the *Morning Chronicle,* the *States and Union,* the *Daily Evening Times,* and the *Portsmouth Citizen.* Hartford then closed every competing paper, giving his daily *Herald* and his weekly *Gazette* the monopoly on local news. What was good for Portsmouth was good for newspaper circulation to the only publisher in town.

So why not, Hartford suggested, have the governors of Utah, Iowa, Missouri, Vermont, Minnesota, West Virginia, and New

ABOVE: *This fountain decorated with dolphins survives, in part, from Beckwith's collection. (ATH)*

Hampshire travel from Connecticut by naval destroyer to Portsmouth? Then they could stay at the Wentworth and travel to the mountains by train. Alabama, North Carolina, and Oklahoma, who had sent lesser representatives, could come along for the ride. And so it was. Unfortunately, New York Governor Franklin Delano Roosevelt, who knew the Wentworth from his visits to Portsmouth as former assistant secretary of the Navy, did not attend—even after Hartford had reported otherwise in the *Herald*. The other governors arrived on the battleship *U.S.S. Toucey* from New London, toured the Navy Yard, and dined on squab and lobster at the Wentworth. The following day they took a special train to the White Mountains, where *Old Peppersass* indiscreetly broke a cog and careened off the tracks at the base of New England's tallest peak during the dedication ceremony.

In his waning years, Hartford grew nostalgic for bygone days at the old Victorian hotel. In the late 1920s he wrote a number of unsigned, but clearly distinguishable, articles. In one, Hartford toured the hotel with Harry Beckwith and credits the Wentworth as having exerted a powerful influence on the growth and reputation of the region:

> What a great hotel like the Wentworth means to historic Portsmouth and picturesque New Castle is, we believe, hardly appreciated or understood by most people. The reputation of such a hotel means the widest kind of publicity of the sort that tends to build up a community like ours to the farthermost points of the country. It is of as much value as any industry of like size in the number of men and women employed. How many of our citizens have met Proprietor Harry Beckwith and really appreciated and understood what he has built and is building?

When New York Governor Franklin D. Roosevelt and his rambunctious sons arrived at Little Harbor aboard his sailboat *Myth II* in July 1932, among the first visitors to scramble aboard the yacht was the rotund Portsmouth mayor and *Herald* editor Fernando W. Hartford. Roosevelt had just been nominated as

OPPOSITE TOP: *Self-effacing hotel employees await the arrival of guests for tea. Many Wentworth staff members migrated from the Carolina at Pinehurst, North Carolina, year after year, keeping the same position and duties. (ATH)*

OPPOSITE BOTTOM: *Well-behaved young guests improve their minds in a quiet corner of the piazza. (ATH)*

the presidential candidate for the Democratic Party and, despite his opposing politics, Hartford had his photo taken with the candidate aboard ship. When Roosevelt came ashore the next day he was greeted by Harry Beckwith, who reportedly said, "Governor, there is the Hotel Wentworth, which is yours during your stay, for you and your friends."

Candidate Roosevelt, according to the newspaper account, then walked to the hotel and signed the register, but without going in. Then he said, "If you will look back to the year 1919, you will find my signature in the register."

By noon crowds anticipating Roosevelt's two o'clock public address had already crammed Market Square in Portsmouth, filling Pleasant Street as far back as State Street. People wanted to see, rather than hear, the famous relative of Teddy Roosevelt, the *Herald* noted, as if viewing royalty rather than a politician. After touring Portsmouth with Mayor Hartford, Roosevelt's entourage traveled down the coast to Hampton Beach, as had President Chester A. Arthur in the early days of the hotel, where crowds of July beachgoers angled for a view.

A year later Roosevelt, then president of the United States, again sailed past the Republican-dominated Wentworth and anchored in Little Harbor. Again Fernando W. Hartford, now a former mayor but still *Herald* editor, was among the first aboard—and he came bearing gifts. According to the newspaper report, Hartford gave President Roosevelt three books, all popular with seacoast history buffs today. FDR received a deluxe edition of the recently published *Ninety Years at the Isles of Shoals,* by poet Celia Thaxter's brother Oscar Laighton; an original nineteenth-century copy of Charles Brewster's *Rambles About Portsmouth;* and the ever-popular hardcover tour guide by Caleb Gurney, *Portsmouth: Historic and Picturesque.*

Roosevelt never left the *Amberjack II,* though he waved to onlookers who gathered on the shore and floated at a respectable distance in every sort of watercraft until well after dusk. He and his sons sailed off the next morning, but not before the *Herald* could squeeze in one more plug for its aging editor and his favorite hotel:

When James Roosevelt returned to the Wentworth House dock this morning, he greeted Former Mayor Hartford with these words, "Father certainly enjoyed those books about Portsmouth and the Isles of Shoals. He stayed up late to read much of the interesting history."

Anyone observing the yachts and lawn parties and luxury automobiles on any summer day at Wentworth by the Sea could easily forget the crushing poverty that prevailed across so much of America in the 1930s. But not everyone in the nation was destitute or struggling to make ends meet. Wealthy hotel guests were busy modeling for one another at style shows, dressing up in Gay Nineties regalia, or attending a costume ball dressed as victims of a shipwreck. Memorable guests from the Beckwith era included U.S. Supreme Court Chief Justice Charles Evans Hughes. Famed Broadway actress Edith Barrett was among the theater cast at the Ship. With writer Booth Tarkington and other dignitaries in the audience, Barrett performed a comedy by *Winnie the Pooh* author A. A. Milne. Barrett's distinguished Broadway career took a tumble when she moved to film and appeared in the kitsch classic *I Walked with a Zombie*.

One of the most extravagant Hollywood films of the era may have been modeled on life at the Wentworth. Busby Berkeley's lush musical Gold Diggers of 1935 parodies the interplay between wealthy hotel guests and the hardworking army of summer staff. Of course, love crosses the poverty line as a Pittsfield, Massachusetts, socialite, heiress to a $10 million flypaper manufacturing company, falls for the hotel's head clerk. Released smack in the middle of the Depression under FDR, the film opens with a hobo in frayed tophat, tie, and tails reading a classy magazine. The camera zooms in on an advertisement for The Wentworth Plaza, "a name synonymous with luxury living." The fictional resort is located, not on the sea, but at Lake Waxapahachie, New Hampshire, clearly derived from nearby Lake Winnipesaukee. A manager, looking very much like Harry Beckwith, greets his summer staff with the following speech:

> You are here to serve the most exacting clientele of any
> hotel in America, in the world. The Wentworth Plaza,

ABOVE: *Two supposed Wentworth by the Sea guests, Herbert Hoover and Franklin Delano Roosevelt, attend to more weighty political matters in Washington, D.C. (LIB)*

as you know, caters only to the most exclusive and the wealthiest guests. You are the temporary servants of those who demand the most of their servants, and yet some of you receive no salaries. That is because I could never begin to pay you what you will earn in honoraria—I mean tips.

The film pokes fun at the practice in which staff members pooled their tips. A large percentage of that income went into the pockets of the headwaiter, head bellman, the head housekeeper, and the head clerk. The Wentworth motto, according to the film version is—"The guest is always right, even though he is wrong—because he pays."

The film features classic pop hits including "I'm Going Shopping with You," "The Forgotten Man," and "The Lullaby of Broadway." The climactic choreography features a surreal chorus of women playing forty white grand pianos that float around the screen with kaleidoscopic precision.

But millionaires could be cheapskates, as the Busby Berkeley film implies. Wentworth owner James Smith often recounted anecdotal proof. He wrote in his short memoir about the CEO of one of the nation's largest oil companies, who was scandalized by the marked-up price of newspapers sold at the Wentworth. Rather than pay eight cents, the CEO send his chauffeur three miles to Portsmouth each day to pick up the paper for a nickel.

Olive Tardiff, an Exeter historian who worked as a "college girl" Wentworth waitress in 1935, recalls a story that says volumes about this era.

> The best tip I ever remember getting was from a little old lady who was dressed in black, always black old-fashioned clothes. She was probably about eighty, I would guess, and very liberal-minded. Not liberated, but liberal-minded because she insisted on having her chauffeur and maid eat at the same table with her. I don't know how I wound up with her, unless [the management] thought the maid and chauffeur shouldn't be on the better side of the room, so they put her over in

OPPOSITE: *The Hollywood film extravaganza* Gold Diggers of 1935 *takes place at a fictional Wentworth Plaza in New Hampshire. Directed and choreographed by Busby Berkeley, the film parodies the relationship between poor hotel workers and rich hotel guests at the height of the Great Depression. (JDR)*

a corner where I was waiting on tables. They really didn't want to eat there. They would have much preferred to eat out in the dining room with the other chauffeurs and maids, but she felt she was doing them a favor, showing them how generous she was. So they stayed a week . . . and she tipped me ten dollars, and that was the most I ever got.

Madeline Thomson, another summer waitress, recalled the Beckwith era to author Raymond Brighton in 1987. Employees, she said, danced and romanced every Wednesday evening at their own crude "Mosquito Hall" out by the old dormitories and the motorcar garage. Thomson summed up the hotel this way:

> It was an elegant place. It gave me a foundation for poise, manners, etiquette by just watching the people, because they were all essentially beautiful people—but strictly, for all that, they were Republicans.

But the golden days were fleeting. The distant engines of war were revving up again and would soon put an end to the summerlong party. Submarine production at the Navy Yard, reduced to only a single new vessel every other year, now throttled forward to four new ships in 1939. Among those four was the famous *Squalus,* which went missing during its maiden voyage just off the Isles of Shoals. Thirty-three men trapped in the forward compartment were saved using an experimental diving bell in the nation's only successful submarine rescue. Later, the salvaged sub with the bodies of twenty-six others was floated to the surface. Wentworth by the Sea gardener Alice Hackney recalled watching from the hotel grounds as the *Squalus* broke the surface, faltered, and sank again seconds later. After several attempts, the submarine was recovered and later recommissioned as the *U.S.S. Sailfish.*

But despite the tragedy, Portsmouth profited as war loomed. The shipyard was at full capacity as Hitler ravaged Europe. Unable to travel abroad, visitors packed into Wentworth by the Sea through the summer of 1941, even as troops continued to build at three New Castle military bases just a stone's throw down the road. Then Pearl Harbor changed everything. The

OPPOSITE: *A page from an advertising brochure in the 1930s offers a glimpse of the period furnishings in a number of the hotel's public rooms. (ATH)*

federal government took over the Odiorne family farm and lands directly across from the hotel. The land where David Thompson had built his 1623 palisade fort against Indian attack was torn up and transformed into deep bunkers, ammunition caches, and gun batteries to ward off Nazi and Japanese invaders. The Wentworth was surrounded on both sides by military camps set to defend the Portsmouth Naval Shipyard, which manufactured scores of submarines over the next four years.

The Wentworth management announced on March 31, 1942, that, for the safety of its patrons, Wentworth by the Sea would not open for the first time in seventy years. Military officials took over the hotel's dormitories, garages, and stable and eventually the golf course. Everyone and everything in the seacoast was now refitted for war. On Thursday, June 22, 1944, Portsmouth Harbor shuddered with an explosion not felt since the dynamiting at Henderson's Point in 1905. Army officials were testing the heavy-caliber guns in the Portsmouth Harbor Defense Program. Ceiling plaster fell from a New Castle house and nearby a number of windows in the empty Wentworth shattered from the shock waves of the artillery fire.

A popular but inaccurate legend holds that Wentworth by the Sea was painted black during the war to disguise it from enemy attack. Closed for two years, the great white hotel was "dimmed," or "blacked out" by having the lights shut off during two inactive summers. Rumors that the Army ran a top-secret operation there appear equally unfounded.

In Texas, meanwhile, home on a brief leave after two years of war, a lanky young Army Air Corps officer named Jim kissed his wife, Bessie, good-bye again and returned to his duties in Florida. Someday, when the war was over, they promised each other, they would run their own hotel.

OPPOSITE TOP: *The test firing of the heavy artillery guns at Fort Dearborn in Rye signaled the arrival of another world war. The hotel closed for two years in 1943 and 1944, but reopened under new young managers. (SSC)*

OPPOSITE BOTTOM: *In 1939, during the* Squalus *salvage operation, the submarine broke the surface as shown here, only to become unstable and sink again. This photo was taken months after the daring rescue of the thirty-three survivors in May. (ATH)*

# Margaret and Jim

James Barker Smith met Margaret Tasher in the spring of 1927. She passed him in the college quadrangle at the University of Colorado at Boulder on her way to the gym. He was among the tallest men on campus and she was the only female among a class of three hundred. From that chance encounter came a Wentworth team that would outlast the first four owners and their many managers combined.

Jim Smith's father and grandfather were hotel men through and through. When they learned that Elsworth Milton Statler had begun the nation's first hotel administration program at Cornell University, they insisted that Jim, who was halfway through college in Colorado Springs, transfer to New York and start over as a freshman. He did, and spent summers interning at top Colorado hotels. He graduated directly into the Great Depression, a bad time for the luxury-hotel business. After knocking about for two years without a job, Jim landed a prestigious management position at the Broadmoor at the foot of the Rocky Mountains in Colorado. The couple married and joined a fast-moving social set in the evolving resort community. Margaret became the first woman to ski from the top of Pike's Peak—before there was even a trail.

The Smiths were on a roll. Five years later, in 1939, they left the Broadmoor for the Plaza Hotel in Houston, Texas, and Jim Smith's whopping $350 a month salary, plus free room and board. Then came tragedy. In the fall of 1941 a daughter died soon after

ABOVE: *The new hotel owners move East in the 1940s. (ATH)*

OPPOSITE: *James and Margaret Smith join the hoedown soon after their purchase of Wentworth by the Sea. (ATH)*

birth. Scores of sympathy letters and telegrams flooded in from a wide circle of young friends. As the couple were recovering from their loss, the Japanese attacked Pearl Harbor.

Jim joined the Army and was commissioned as a first lieutenant at Eglin Air Force Base in Florida, where he managed the officers club. Margaret took over her husband's job as hotel manager in Houston. While many women went to work during the war, then returned to domestic life, Margaret Smith was no temp. Despite Jim's hotel administration degree, few who knew the Smiths ever questioned that Margaret was the financial wizard and a full partner. Jim's convivial style and professional training were the ideal balance to Margaret's rock-solid, take-no-prisoners management instincts.

In 1943 Margaret gave birth to their son, James Jr. She was soon back at work, balancing motherhood with her job at the Plaza. Margaret worked sometimes seven days a week, a pattern she repeated for nearly four decades. Through the war, in constant letters and phone calls, she kept her husband up to date on the smallest of hotel details, even sending regular financial reports for his review.

From the start they had talked about owning their own hotel. Motels were the current rage. Cheap new roadside shelters, little more than wood frames and canvas tops, were available for fifty cents a night. But even with Jim in Florida and with a war on, their conversation focused on buying a refined and luxurious hotel. In the summer of 1945, as the end of hostilities drew near, Jim spied an advertisement in the *New York Times* for a Maine hotel for sale. He made a quick trip, his first ever to New England, from the Army base at Fort Walton, Florida. But real estate agent Arthur Langdon had an even hotter tip: The famous Wentworth had come on the market the day before. It had recently reopened to guests after two dormant years, though without fanfare, and Langdon suggested a detour to New Hampshire. On July third, a lanky Major James Barker Smith got his first view of the aging Victorian hotel. He told reporters four decades later:

> It was love at first sight. When I entered the dining room, I was the only man in the room that didn't have

ABOVE: *For a brief period after purchasing the Wentworth in 1946, the young James Barker Smith preferred that employees address him as "Major." (ATH)*

a dinner jacket on. I had on a uniform, of course. The women were so resplendent in their silks and their satins and diamonds and pearls.

The Smiths never tired of reminding each other how close they came to not owning the Wentworth. It was Labor Day, the end of the tourist season, before Margaret could find the time to slip away from the Plaza and make a quick trip east. Timing was everything. Within hours of the last departing summer guest, the Wentworth would be buttoned up tight until the following year. Margaret caught a plane from Houston to New York. The train from there to Boston was so crowded, she recalled, that she had to stand in the vestibule the entire way. The couple was supposed to meet at the Parker House before the short trip to New Hampshire, but Jim did not arrive. No word came by dinner, or all through the night. The next morning Margaret was sitting nervously in a car with the real estate agent ready to depart for New Castle when she made one last desperate trip to see the hotel desk clerk. This time the clerk found a telegram from Jim, sent the day before, but never delivered. Jim's flight from Eglin Airfield had been delayed, the message said. Margaret should instead pick him up at Hanscom Field outside Boston. But when Margaret didn't arrive, Jim had taken a taxi into Boston to search for her. By the time Margaret called officials at Hanscom, Jim was already gone—she assumed to New Hampshire. When he got to the Parker House, she had just left. Margaret was still sitting in the dining room of the Wentworth at three P.M. in the final cliffhanging hours on the last day of the summer season when the handsome Major Smith stepped through the doors like the leading man in a Hollywood film. They were reunited at last. And Margaret was already smitten. She, too, had fallen deeply in love with their new summer home.

It was a good deal. Harry Beckwith, a manufacturer at heart, was weary of the hotel trade and asking a flat $200,000. That was a tidy sum for the Smiths, just back together after three years. Jim offered $40,000 cash with Beckwith assuming the mortgage, then $70,000, then more. Smith continually requested detailed financial records, but Beckwith sent along only brief

ABOVE: *While Major Smith served out the war years in Florida, Margaret Tasker Smith managed the Plaza Hotel in Houston, in his absence. This photo is signed "Dear Jim, I love you. Bessie." (ATH)*

notes and stuck to his price. By March the Smiths had pulled together the funds and sealed the deal. The cost included the sprawling 256-room hotel, all its dormitories and outbuildings, the Ship and tidal swimming pool, the golf course, plus Harry Beckwith's house on the water just across the little bridge below the hotel, plus several hundred more acres in Rye and New Castle. As a bonus, the Smiths inherited the hotel's sterling reputation and seventy-two-year history.

According to Beckwith's letters to Jim Smith, the hotel grossed about $180,000 in the war years and made an annual profit of only $5,000 to $10,000. "As you know," Beckwith wrote the Smiths in August 1945, "we have never tried to operate on a profit basis due to the fact that our other business interests took care of the profits…"

Not so for James and Margaret. They increased gross income by $100,000 their first season in 1946. The strategy was classic hotel school good sense—expand the seasons and slowly raise prices to increase revenue, give customers the best experience possible, and plow back every dollar earned into renovating and improving the giant resort. Smith told Ray Brighton that he paid himself $20,000 a year as the owner. Margaret earned $10,000, but she didn't even take that during the start-up years of the 1940s. Jim insists they stuck to that formula throughout their careers, quickly raising the gross hotel income to $7 million per season. Each year $250,000 was budgeted to make repairs and upgrades to the hotel and campus. Although exact figures were not revealed, sale of the hotel in 1982 has been estimated at $5.8 million.

There is no doubt that the Smiths knew they were purchasing an "exclusive" hotel. Harry Beckwith had written them in 1945, "We have a fine clientele, and even during the depression years, we kept it select." A few months later, when another resort they were considering in Maine was sold to a Jewish buyer, the real estate agent wrote to Jim Smith, "This makes the Wentworth so much better because now there is one less first-class large resort that is restricted in New England."

It was a turnkey operation. Wentworth by the Sea came complete with everything from bed linens to a trained staff.

What the Smiths announced as sweeping new improvements in 1946 were a return to the policies of the hotel in its heyday before the war—more fine cuisine, efficient services, live entertainment, grand parties, and the usual golf, tennis, boating, fishing, swimming, and horseback riding.

While absentee owners Beckwith, Jones, and Chase had largely been investors with other sources of income, the hands-on Smiths owed their living almost entirely to the Wentworth. They quickly inched up room rates and added a dollar to a dining plan that offered three hearty gourmet meals for eight dollars per person per day. That was still a bargain. A 1948 news report noted that restaurant prices immediately after the war were up as much as seventy-eight percent over the year before. Consistent as the tides, the Smiths continued to raise the rates one dollar every year.

Even before the hotel opened that first season, according to a *Herald* news release, the Kansas- and Colorado-born owners had managed to book twenty private functions ahead of the July season. In time, according to Smith, the Wentworth came to host an average of 250 major functions annually, from conferences, to banquets, to weddings. They expanded the spring and fall shoulder conference seasons to include much of May and October, creating three distinct sub-seasons with the short July-to-August New Hampshire tourist summer in the middle.

Entertainment was crucial. Modern visitors no longer arrived with steamer trunks, maids, and chauffeurs in search of a long summer rest. Short-stay vacationers wanted things to do every day and every night. The Smith approach crystallized the traditional Wentworth evening activities into a strict calendar that repeated itself wcck after week, decade after decade. Besides nightly dancing and an endless schedule of performances, games, parties, and get-togethers, the evening calendar included:

| | |
|---|---|
| Monday: | Newcomer's Cocktail Party followed by bingo |
| Tuesday: | New movie at the Ship |
| Wednesday: | Ballroom dancing with Bob Brunton's orchestra |
| Thursday: | New movie at the Ship and bridge parties |
| Friday: | Square dancing |

ABOVE: *The Smiths pose with previous Wentworth by the Sea owner Harry Beckwith years after they purchased the resort for $200,000. (ATH)*

ABOVE: *"The Ship" remained active as theater, lounge, movie house, and party center throughout the Smith era. The saltwater pool was replaced by a modern facility in the mid-'60s. (ATH).*

| Saturday: | Gala dress-up with dinner and ballroom dancing |
|---|---|
| Sunday: | Concert by Wentworth Symphonetta, then a lecture |

The Wentworth became a central booking agency for local talent. Jim Smith was always on the lookout for new performers, from exotic Hawaiian dancers, to racing turtles, to a dog that could reportedly do arithmetic. The Smiths employed a family of entertainers, many of whom returned for decades. There was a square dance caller, ballroom dancers doubling as dance instructors, musicians, a house sketch artist, and a staff photographer.

On a trip to New Hampshire's Mount Washington resort, Smith lured singers Dick and Genie Court back to Portsmouth, where they have lived ever since. When not performing at the Wentworth, they booked talent for the endless parade of conferences, private guest "socials," evening events, and weddings. Performers ranged from the likes of Cab Calloway and Duke Ellington to a ten-year-old girl who wandered among guests playing an accordion. Acts were booked and records were kept on slips of paper and pasted together into weekly schedules. Genie Court remembers, a system that was not always flawless:

"One weekend we had fourteen different groups at the same time, anywhere from twenty to four hundred people," she says. "Things would get lost occasionally. There were times when a bus of forty-eight people would pull up at the hotel and nobody knew they were coming."

There was something magical about dressing up. The Smiths were especially fond of the Saturday-night galas that harkened back to the "good old days" of Frank Jones. Second best was any excuse to wear costumes at a masquerade or Mardi Gras. Margaret kept at least four hundred costumes at the ready, but guests often drove great distances to rent the best outfits for the festivities.

The biggest masquerade ball came at the end of the season and was followed, as tradition dictated, by the employee bash. Frank Graham was a meat cutter in the kitchen during the Smiths' first season in 1946. He recalls the employee masquerade with its lingering postwar giddiness. Graham says he had no

ABOVE: *The Smiths provided continuous entertainment for guests and conventioneers. Many of the entertainers returned for years, some for decades—including singers Dick and Genie Court and square dancers Jean and Arthur Tufts of Exeter. Pictured here are Nino and Helen Settineri, who performed and taught ballroom dancing. (ATH)*

money for a costume, so he borrowed a pair of boots from a stable hand, slicked back his hair, and dabbed on a shoe-polish mustache. Dressed as the recently defeated Adolf Hitler, he quickly coupled with a woman masquerading as Eva Braun. When the dance band asked if anyone wished to sing, Graham gave a stirring rendition of "Hitler in the Snow," to the tune of "Turkey in the Straw." The bizarre scene was captured by a local news photographer.

Graham had made the newspapers earlier that season, too. While preparing three hundred ducks for roasting at a fancy Wentworth banquet, he had discovered a four-legged duck. That was excuse enough to get a cameraman out to the Wentworth kitchen, and for the rest of their tenure the Smiths kept a professional photographer on hand. The Smiths' massive archive of photographs in the Portsmouth Athenaeum show guests in every situation—from formal dancing to racing turtles. The collection documents the waning years of the century-old summering society. Crew-cut boys in madras sport coats square dance with girls in horn-rimmed glasses. Each scene seems cut from an episode of *Ozzie and Harriet* or *Leave It to Beaver* and played out against an ornate senior prom set. Always at the forefront, the three Smiths masquerade as veterans of the Civil War, gangsters, cowboys, Mexican peasants, turbaned Indian rajas, and more. In one shot, a bearded hillbilly Smith leads his son into the ballroom astride a small burro.

Second only to dressing up, Jim Smith's greatest passion was dressing down opponents on the tennis courts. In the 1890s the Wentworth hosted, with the exception of Newport, Rhode Island, the ultimate New England tennis tournament, the predecessor of today's prestigious matches. Under Harry Beckwith, however, the game had taken a back seat to swimming and golf. Within days of purchasing the hotel, Smith began a very public campaign to restore the sport. He offered free tennis instruction to local kids, improved the hotel's two clay courts and eventually added five more courts. He set up high-profile tournaments and attracted even more media attention by matching octogenarian players with twelve-year-old girls to demonstrate the wide age range possible in this versatile game.

ABOVE: *Frank Graham, dressed as Hitler, marches just behind the Invisible Man at the 1946 employee masquerade ball. (FG)*

OPPOSITE: *Over three decades the Smiths donned many costumes. Margaret kept more than four hundred outfits available for guests. (ATH)*

He also found a lifetime partner in Wadleigh Woods, the son of major-league baseball star Wally Woods of Portsmouth. According to Wentworth legend, the new hotel owner challenged Woods to a shootout in 1946. Beat me, Smith offered, and you're hired. Woods did, and managed tennis at Wentworth by the Sea for thirty-four consecutive summers. At the end of each long day, Woods recalled in a later interview, just as he was getting ready to go home, Jim Smith would arrive, racket in hand, psyched for an early-evening match. A longstanding challenge was then issued—guests who defeated the dynamic duo of Woods and Smith received free room and board at the hotel. It happened only twice.

In their very first season, Smith and Woods invited eleven touring tennis pros to an exhibition match for a group fee of a thousand dollars. In the first doubles round the Wentworth team—the new owner and his new wonder boy—challenged top professionals Bobby Riggs and Welby Van Horn. The game was so exciting and the score so close that local sportswriters ecstatically spread the story. The resulting ink went a long way to reinvigorating the game in New Hampshire.

"They were kind to us," Smith later said, "and made it look like a highly contested match."

Though clearly out of his league, Woods agreed to face the top pro in a singles match. The next day a local headline shouted "Wadleigh Woods Forces Riggs in Wentworth Opener."

"Mostly, I wanted to be able to say I once played Bobby Riggs," Woods told historian Ray Brighton forty years later. "Well, he made me look good and he did it so skillfully that no one in the crowd was the wiser."

Although it could not top the 1905 peace treaty, the Smiths did make the history books early in their career as hosts to the National Governor's Conference. New Hampshire governor Charles M. Dale just happened to be from Portsmouth. The governor of Maine just happened to be the event chairman, but when no "downeast" facility could offer the size and accessibility of the Wentworth, a deal was struck. America was enjoying a boom, not just in postwar babies, but in the economy as well. Sixty shiny new Ford cars, one for use by each of the governors

ABOVE: *Tennis pro Wadleigh Woods served up lessons for Wentworth guests throughout the thirty-four years the Smiths owned the hotel. A schoolteacher off-season, Woods died at age ninety-five the year before the hotel reopened.* (ATH)

and other VIPs, were lined up in the Wentworth garage as the dignitaries arrived. The gigantic aircraft carrier *U.S.S. Saipan* loomed protectively offshore as the national media set up a communications room inside the hotel. Equally prepared, Jim Smith booked both the Rockingham Hotel and the Harrington in Rye to handle any overflow.

One of the premier moments in Jim Smith's management career occurred as the conference opened and New York governor Thomas E. Dewey made his much anticipated arrival. Dewey was, according to the conventional wisdom of the day, a virtual shoo-in to defeat mild-mannered Harry S. Truman for president in the approaching election. According to Brighton, then a cub reporter, Dewey's black limousine wheeled up to the Wentworth entrance in mid-afternoon on June 13. The future leader of the free world shook hands with Governor Dale, then shook hands with his likely Republican presidential challenger Governor Earl Warren and asked, "What's doing tonight?" When Dale said nothing much was planned, Dewey replied, "Good, maybe we can get a good night's sleep tonight."

Nobody wanted to get on the wrong side of Dewey. But the governor was not happy with his room. A bipartisan committee had made all the room assignments, but Dewey, who brought along his wife and two sons, wanted connecting rooms, not a suite of adjoining rooms, for his family. Although Jim Smith did not have the authority to redesign the master room plan, he rushed into the fray only to hear Governor Dewey utter the most horrible words imaginable: "Mr. Smith, someone has erred colossally. I couldn't stay here overnight!" "At that moment I was in rather a panic because the hotel was filled," Smith later recalled. "He was the last to come, I thought. I scooted down to the front office, and Lord, there was one suite left in the whole hotel. Governor Strom Thurmond of South Carolina, who had not arrived yet, had the connecting rooms. I quickly took the keys to the suite and was back there in two minutes, I believe. Dewey said—'That is the quickest change I ever saw at a hotel.'"

Dewey, of course, was defeated for president and is best remembered as the man who counted his chickens before they hatched. Others, however, went on to bigger things. Strom

ABOVE: *A guest waits for a court in this publicity photograph from the extensive Friends of the Wentworth archive in the Portsmouth Athenaeum. (ATH)*

Thurmond survived to become, at age one hundred, the oldest sitting U.S. senator. Earl Warren became chief justice of the Supreme Court and gave his name to the Warren Commission Report on the assassination of President John F. Kennedy. On-the-scene reporter Raymond Brighton, who had his picture taken with Warren, whom he greatly admired, became editor of the *Portsmouth Herald*.

The nation's governors feasted on Mississippi shrimp, poached Maine salmon, and larded tenderloin of beef. They listened to reporter Edward R. Murrow's lecture, "America as an Island." Smith recalled another near fiasco from the 1948 Governor's Conference when the entire group gathered by the water's edge to enjoy one of the famous Wentworth by the Sea clambakes. The weekly "bakes" on the southern island beach were legendary. A fire pit filled with wood burned all day. Lobsters, clams, fish, and corn steamed in layers of seaweed under a canvas cover. At its peak, counting hotel guests, visitors, and conference attendees, long lines of diners might consume a thousand lobsters in a day under chief cook Alfred Meloon.

In 1948 the governors and their wives were elegantly dressed, having already attended a formal cocktail reception at the Portsmouth Naval Shipyard. The weather was threatening, but Smith had sent home the entire kitchen staff. Just as the lobsters, clam chowder, and corn were served in cardboard carry boxes, the clouds burst into a drenching rain. Smith wrote in a short memoir:

> Everybody threw all the food on the ground in order to hold the empty boxes over their heads. We rushed back to the hotel . . . In the kitchen was one employee only, and he was busy polishing silver. Nevertheless, many of the governors and their wives pitched in and roasted hotdogs, heated rolls and made coffee. Before long all were in good humor, and the fourth estate had a good story for the morning newspapers.

Newspaper readers were not allowed to see press photos of Governor Dewey soaking wet. According to Brighton, aides to Governor Dale blocked the cameras. It wasn't expedient for

ABOVE: *Jim Smith plays post office at the hotel. (ATH)*

OPPOSITE: *James Smith and Thomas E. Dewey at the historic Governor's Conference in 1948. Many considered Dewey a shoo-in for president in the upcoming election against Harry Truman. History proved otherwise. (ATH)*

people across the nation to know that it rained in New Hampshire or that their potential president was less than waterproof. Late that evening, while making a final check of the hotel, Smith discovered Governor Dewey with his head in the Wentworth kitchen refrigerator searching out a midnight snack.

Jim Smith became a federal employee himself the following year, in 1949, when he was sworn in as "postmaster" at the hotel. Technically, it was not an official position, but rather a contract he cleverly negotiated with the New Castle post office. The agreement allowed the hotel to stamp postcards with the Wentworth name. Official or not, it generated plenty of free publicity. Another marketing boon had come the year before, in 1948, when the Smiths expanded their holdings and purchased the Rockingham in Portsmouth for roughly $100,000. It was the first time the sister hotels had been under the same ownership in forty-one years.

Jim Smith never mentioned on the record the event that later earned the Rockingham a spot on the Portsmouth Black Heritage Trail. In 1948 Smith came head-to-head with documentary filmmaker Louis de Rochemont, best known for his *March of Time* newsreels seen monthly by millions of moviegoers from 1936 to 1951. An anti-Hollywood maverick, de Rochemont settled in the nearby town of Newington and produced a number of successful independent films after the war, among them the controversial *Lost Boundaries.* The plot centered on a light-skinned African-American family "passing" for white in New Hampshire. It was one of the nation's first films to focus on racial issues. Although the stars, Mel Ferrer and Beatrice Pearson, were white, there were many blacks in the supporting cast. De Rochemont made the Rockingham his headquarters for the filming in 1948. When owner Smith refused to allow black cast members to eat or attend meetings in the hotel, de Rochemont threatened to move his entire costly film production elsewhere. Smith relented and the Rockingham was promptly integrated.

But it was not until 1964 that the Wentworth followed suit. Following enactment of legislation that year, a number of civil rights volunteers, black and white, methodically put new antisegregation legislation to the test. On July 4, a University of New Hampshire professor and his wife made reservations for four at the Wentworth dining room and paid for the meals in advance. The white couple arrived first and, as expected, when the second couple turned out to be African-American, they were denied access to the public restaurant. The couple who had made the reservations were called into the owner's office and, according to their handwritten report, an extremely uncomfortable conversation followed. All four members of the group were asked to leave. They would prefer instead, they told the owner, to use his telephone to call the police and report the infraction of the civil rights law. The "sting" succeeded. Apologies were made all around, and the group returned to the dining room for the hotel's first integrated evening.

Years earlier, when confronted with another sticky political dilemma, James Smith had used more tact. During the "Red" scare in 1950, Senator Joseph McCarthy and Vice President Richard Nixon saw Communists lurking under every bush. That summer Johns Hopkins professor Owen Lattimore dined at the Wentworth as the guest of William G. Wendell, a member of a prominent Portsmouth family. When the blue bloods attending dinner that evening learned that Lattimore, a target of McCarthy, was planning to speak on foreign relations, a protest arose. Smith decided to poll those in attendance and suggested that Mr. Lattimore could speak if seventy-five percent of those in attendance agreed. Of the 350 guests polled, 140 refused to cast ballots, and 121 voted against the scholar. Lattimore did not hit Smith's required quota and he did not speak.

A staunch supporter of local business, James Barker Smith was best known for his charitable work as a loyal Rotarian. The Smiths believed in buying local produce, hiring local people, and supporting local causes. But when faced with policies that threatened the hotel's bottom line, Jim let his opinions fly. He vehemently opposed the institution of a minimum wage for employees in 1949, predicting that the passage of a proposed seventy-five-cents-per-hour rate would bankrupt the hotel industry within five years. The law passed at a lowered minimum rate of fifty cents, but did not apply to many hospitality workers

ABOVE: *Margaret and Sen. Edward Brooke of Massachusetts, who appeared on the cover of* Time *magazine in 1967. (ATH)*

receiving tips. Smith later protested that Wentworth by the Sea would not survive the passage of New Hampshire's proposed room and meals tax—he called it the "bed and belly tax"—but the tax passed and the hotel thrived.

The owner's ongoing battle with New Castle police chief Henry Greenberg plays, in retrospect, like a television sitcom. Beginning in 1952, Greenberg set his sights on hotel guests who parked alongside the small rural road that passed the hotel. Each ticket, which Smith himself paid for his guests, was like a stinging projectile. When Greenberg ticketed the shiny new fire trucks during the annual New England Fire Chiefs Convention, Smith was aghast. But the best was yet to come.

On Saturday, August 27, 1960, on a tip from a guest at the hotel, the New Castle police under Chief Greenberg and a state trooper raided the the Ship at Wentworth by the Sea on charges of operating an illegal gambling site. Two employees were arrested and, according to one eyewitness, a lot of prestigious, well-dressed guests who could not afford to be taken into custody ran for the hills. The controversy hovered around a used slot machine that Margaret Smith had purchased in Florida and added to the festivities of the annual Casino Night theme party. Police confiscated $52.35 in coins as evidence. They later fined one employee twenty-five dollars and revoked the hotel's liquor license for ten days. But that license didn't stay revoked for long. "We got it back," Margaret Smith remembered, "because our next convention was a police convention, and they had to have a bar."

Jim Smith got his revenge. To pay for public education without a state income tax, the Granite State enacted a Sweepstakes Commission and sold "sweeps" tickets in automated vending machines. Two of the machines were located in the Wentworth lobby. When the dreaded "bed and belly tax" passed the New Hampshire legislature in 1967, in a highly public protest, Smith ordered the state-sanctioned gambling machines removed from his hotel. The governor refused to put them back even when Smith admitted he had perhaps reacted "a little hastily."

Despite stormy politics, the Smith years were profitable ones for Wentworth by the Sea. By 1962, son James Barker Smith Jr. had himself graduated from hotel school and became part of the Smith family team. As construction manager, Jim Jr. adapted the historic Donald Ross golf course into a full eighteen-hole facility and expanded the clubhouse. Locals, according to historian Brighton, could at one time play a full round after work for fifty cents. A modern, Olympic-sized pool replaced the aging saltwater pool just above the Ship, which was itself enlarged. For young New Castle natives, the new pool was just another exclusive luxury closed to locals. Resident Richard Morrill remembers that, after shooting rats with BB guns at the Wentworth dump, kids sometimes stole into the saltwater pool at the Ship to cool off. It seemed only fair, Morrill wrote in the *Herald*, since even

ABOVE: *Dancing the night away at the hotel in the swinging 1940s. (ATH)*

in the 1960s when he was growing up, sewage and garbage from the hotel were still dumped directly into Little Harbor. It wasn't uncommon, according to the writer, for boys swimming at the Slide behind the hotel to come to the surface wearing a wad of toilet paper.

The Smiths' renovations, like their politics and sanitation facilities, did not earn them many kudos. Despite what amounted to millions of dollars in remodeling and redecorating, they made no architectural or artistic advances. The now prized Colonial Revival elements were largely destroyed in favor of bland modern construction, contemporary furnishings, and forgettable murals. Rooms were assigned exotic names like Avenida, Cote d'Azure, Capri, and Tally-ho. All the contents would later be sold off in a massive auction.

While most of the work simply kept pace with the fading hotel, under the Smiths the gardens bloomed. For generations the hotel had little more than a front show garden and vegetable and cutting gardens at the rear. Under the Smiths the floral areas were expanded over more than two hundred acres. A new greenhouse and three cold frames were built as early as the 1940s. At one point two thousand rosebushes bloomed among twenty thousand annuals. It was all a great joy to gardener Alice Patch, who had worked the Wentworth since the Frank Jones era. Born in 1870, Patch, with two nieces, rowed a small boat or took the trolley from Kittery, walking the last leg of the journey. Alice Hackney took over when her aunt Alice Patch died in 1956. She was survived by niece Florence Patch Merson, who later worked the hotel gift shop until 1980.

Despite rumors to the contrary, celebrity sightings were few and far between during the Smith era. Actress Gloria Swanson was clearly on the scene. Chicken kings Frank Perdue and Colonel Sanders, columnist Ann Landers, children's TV star Mr. Fred Rogers, and actors Jason Robards and Zero Mostel are among the notables spotted at the hotel during the Smith's period. The archives include a thank-you letter from J. Edgar Hoover for his Wentworth visit in 1950. Vice President Hubert Humphrey visited as, reportedly, did Dan Quayle and presidential hopeful Ralph Nader. Senator Ted Kennedy penned a note to thank his hosts for their well-stocked bar. Prince Charles is rumored to have stayed during his visit to Portsmouth in 1973, but apparently he slept aboard his own ship. The Smiths appear in posed photographs with Herbert Hoover, Margaret Chase Smith, Shirley Temple, Richard Nixon, and others, but the pictures may have been taken at the Flamingo in Miami Beach, or the Rockingham in Portsmouth, or elsewhere.

Economist John Kenneth Galbraith was apparently friendly with the owners, but no one impressed James Smith more than Milton Eisenhower, who became a frequent patron of the hotel. The brother of President Dwight Eisenhower, Milton often stayed in the Smiths' own home, the one purchased from Harry Beckwith. Nicknamed "Margin for Error" by the Smiths, the house was furnished with a half-dozen private guest rooms, attended by hotel staff. The couple routinely overbooked the Wentworth by three percent, so houseguests were common. Milton Eisenhower, a widower, had been actively courted by the Smiths and enjoyed the intimate lodgings. Candid photos show that Margaret often accompanied him on day tours through surrounding New England towns. Eisenhower was eventually president of three universities, including Johns Hopkins.

"His brilliance was breathtaking. His ability to express himself," Smith told Brighton. "Ike said, and I believe it's true, that Milton would have made a better president than him."

The second most favored guest was clearly Ethel Donaghue, a wealthy widow from Connecticut, known for her lavish lifestyle. The elderly multimillionairess delighted in wearing her emeralds, rubies, and diamonds in spectacular displays. Margaret Smith told a *New Hampshire Profiles* reporter that Donaghue once authorized her to spend up to $50,000 catering a private gathering for invited hotel guests. Jim Smith had her in mind when he referred affectionately to his top patrons as "jewel encrusted dowagers" in a 1982 interview in the *Hartford Courant*.

With few exceptions, the Smith years were charmed years too. Winter storms damaged the dock area, as did a small fire on the Wentworth pier, but nothing serious. In 1954 Hurricane Carol blew down three hundred trees, including stately elms.

ABOVE: *During the 1950s, the Smiths also managed the Flamingo Hotel in Miami, and many staff migrated with them. (ATH)*

Always making lemonade from lemons, Jim Smith reasoned that the surrounding trees had probably saved the hotel itself from more-severe damage. A particularly beloved old tree on the golf course lay with its massive roots exposed. Then, ten days later according to witnesses, powerful winds from Hurricane Diane pushed the tree back upright and it survived.

There were seven small fires during the Smith era. But on Fast Day, a former New Hampshire holiday in late April, 1969, their luck ran out. Flames raged through the old wooden garage and dormitories and might have destroyed the main hotel buildings as well if not for a sudden shift in the direction of the wind. One employee, Francis Cull, died in the fire. Cull, a silver polisher, had been seen running back into the dormitory, reportedly to retrieve his wallet, and never came out. With the Smiths from their very first summer, Cull had been the only hotel employee still on the premises the night when the famous Governor's Conference clambake was rained out in 1948. That honor had reportedly earned him two hundred dollars in tips. The morning after the fire, eyes tearing and his voice choked with emotion, Smith announced the tragic news over the hotel's public address system.

Many of the two hundred summer employees left "homeless" by the fire were taken in by local families. Others stayed in makeshift dorms at the military barracks down the road, where new dorms were soon erected. It was, for the Smiths, the saddest day of their lives in New Hampshire.

Jim Smith's coolness under fire contributed to the survival of the Wentworth, observers say, as much as Margaret's business savvy. Patricia S. Cotter, a Wentworth housekeeper for thirty years, recalled a typical incident to the *Herald* in 1992. The Smiths she said, were visiting with VIP guest Frank Perdue, the chicken king, and had asked not to be disturbed. But a crisis arose when another influential guest returned from a round of golf to find his bags missing. With key staff people off duty, Conner was forced to interrupt Smith. Within minutes, Smith had calmed the guest, purchased temporary clothing and toiletries, provided a free meal, and located the guest's bags, which had accidentally been shipped to South Carolina.

ABOVE: *Milton Eisenhower, brother of President Eisenhower, was a frequent and favorite guest at the Smiths' overflow suites known as "Margin for Error." (ATH)*

OPPOSITE: *Just a few of the famous visitors officially photographed at the hotel during the Smith era include (clockwise): Duke Ellington, who performed for summer guests; President Richard Nixon, Prince Charles, and Senator Edward Kennedy. (ATH)*

D20920

But the winds of change were reaching gale force. The year of the fire, 1969, is memorable for youthful uprisings all across the nation as political, sexual, social, and racial revolutions converged. The impact struck hard at "the grand Victorian," where the formal, well-ordered lifestyle was already an anachronism. Susan Chapman Melanson, then a waitress, has turned her memories into a self-published novel about the turbulent summer of '69. According to Melanson, many of the waitstaff requested a weekend off to attend a music festival in Woodstock, New York. Margaret Smith gathered the staff together and announced that, so as not to show favoritism, no staff members would be given leave to go. Hearing that, one by one, half of the kitchen staff abruptly quit. That historic weekend, while half the Wentworth staff was rolling in the mud at Woodstock, the remaining employees catered the annual Antebellum Night in which the Smiths, with their costumed guests and staff, partied to a century-old Civil War theme.

Portsmouth real estate agent Sandy Domina saw it all from the inside. From 1964 to 1971 she worked at the Wentworth as the wife of James Barker Smith Jr. Domina had been coming to the hotel with her family since 1952, when she was nine. She remembers lining up her party dresses in the order in which she would wear them, one for each night of the week. "It was very nice," she says, "in an orderly way. . ."

*ABOVE: In 1969, the most serious fire in the hotel's history broke out in the staff dormitory. An employee of more than two decades was killed when he reentered the building to reclaim his possessions. (ATH)*

*OPPOSITE TOP: The hotel at night in the early Smith years. (DA)*

*OPPOSITE BOTTOM: Dance instructor Jean Tufts leads a class of very young hotel guests during her weekly dance class. (ATH)*

"We were one of the first Catholic families to come into the hotel," Domina says. "It was still very WASP and it was very old money. The dowagers still came up with their trunks and dogs and servants."

Then everything changed. By the mid-'60s, Domina says, there was a sense that the Smiths were struggling to hold their "magical kingdom" together. The old money was running out and the hotel was running down. She recalls Jim Smith carefully targeting clients, like Italian Catholic families in Rhode Island. He would take a stack of three-by-five cards to a motel there, she says, and call until he had booked the coming season. To attract its new Catholic clientele, the Wentworth was now holding Sunday Mass in the ballroom.

Domina remembers an odd incident from the late 1960s that to her symbolized the growing disrespect of young hotel workers for their aging employers. Despite a strict code that barred the waitstaff from removing food from the kitchen, a three-year veteran waitress was caught pilfering. She had hidden a porterhouse steak in her panty hose.

The hotel's traditionally low pay, long hours, and poor living conditions no longer seemed to satisfy the staff. Workers from that era recall taking home forty-five dollars a week after taxes for a forty-eight hour split-shift week. In the dormitories, two showers, perpetually clogged with standing water, might serve twenty residents.

In July 1970 a *Herald* headline reported "Strike at Wentworth." Jim Smith commented that the event was simply "rumblings of a strike" and noted, in classic Smith style, that his employees were "more essential, in a sense, to our hotel than the guests."

That same month, facing rising maintenance and repair costs, the Smiths offered what, in hindsight, was a visionary plan. They asked the town of New Castle for permission to build condominiums on a portion of their land, including the area destroyed by fire. The proposal was the shape of things to come, Smith argued, in an era when large resorts were dying out. A *Herald* editorial taunted New Castle residents opposed to the condo idea, pointing out that the Smiths already had the legal

ABOVE: *Guests received hundreds of trophies for sports and contests and posed for scores of publicity photos. Among all the awards pictured in the archives, this is the largest. (ATH)*

OPPOSITE TOP: *Activities among the rich and famous included the ever-popular spectator sport of turtle racing. (ATH)*

OPPOSITE BOTTOM: *Waitresses and kitchen staff kept hundreds of guests fed. During peak clambake season, as many as 1,000 lobsters were reportedly served in a single day. (ATH)*

right to subdivide and build up to eighty single-family homes on their land. The decision to allow condos, the editorial suggested, was the most important decision the little town had faced since becoming a municipality in 1693. The *Herald* concluded:

> And it's hard to find fault with those who resent any thought of change in their beautiful island surroundings. And who can blame them? They've long been the envy of us lesser beings who dwell on the mainland.

But the condo proposal failed. From the days of David Chase and Charles Campbell, the Wentworth had included a cluster of stand-alone rental cottages. But New Castle was not ready for the scores of luxury condominiums that would inevitably follow. The move that might have invigorated the hotel and saved it from its darkest years was tabled.

In 1973 the Smiths triumphantly celebrated the hotel's hundredth anniversary. It was actually a year too early, but the date neatly coincided with the state's three hundred and fiftieth anniversary and with the visit of bonnie Prince Charles to Portsmouth. Then Wentworth by the Sea settled back into its predictable and profitable rhythm of weddings, banquets, private parties, tournaments, and conferences. For six months each year the breakneck pace continued, but there was now the palpable sense of time winding down.

During the next annual New England Morticians Convention, toastmaster James Barker Smith accepted the hotel microphone as he had so many thousands of times before. "Two weeks ago, Timex was here and brought watches," he told the gathering. "The following week the New England Confectioners were here—and they brought candy. I hope you didn't bring anything."

In the fall of 1980, after thirty-four consecutive summers by the sea, James and Margaret Smith called it quits. Their reign over the magic kingdom was complete and their departure, though regal and well deserved, nearly brought the castle down.

ABOVE: *The party never stopped and everyone danced. (ATH)*

OPPOSITE: *Almost royalty. James Barker and Margaret Smith sold their beloved Wentworth by the Sea hotel in 1980 to a Swiss conglomerate. It remained open for a single year and then closed under a variety of owners until it was rebuilt by Ocean Properties in 2003. (ATH)*

# THE LIMBO YEARS

It was touch-and-go for two watchful decades. Even now, those who kept the long vigil are amazed to see the new hotel alive again with guests and staff. They can admit, at last, that there were times when their hope flagged through six owners and interminable negotiations. They find it difficult to recall the complex chronology of blueprints and promises and tactics and trauma from the day in 1980 when Jim and Margaret Smith sold the Wentworth to the day it reopened in the twenty-first century.

With the departure of the Smiths, the hotel itself appeared to lose heart. The grande dame got an emergency heart transplant in 1981, but the mechanism failed. With the Smiths acting as consultants and their son, James Jr., preparing to take the helm, Wentworth by the Sea opened for what would be its last season for twenty-two years.

The new owner was a Swiss conglomerate. The Pacific Park Corporation was a wholly owned subsidiary of the Berlinger Corporation. Walter Berlinger himself, a major stockholder in SwissAir, flew to New Hampshire to pose for publicity photos with Margaret Smith. Berlinger introduced the Wentworth's interim managers, a Swiss couple who had previously run a hotel in South Africa. The only commercially viable plan, he said, was to run the hotel year-round as a conference and sports center. The renovation, including the purchase price, would cost an estimated $30 million. Although Jim Smith had privately told the

ABOVE: *Most Colonial Revival decorative details were lost when the bulk of the hotel was demolished. (SG)*

OPPOSITE: *A winged headless cherub seems the perfect icon for Wentworth by the Sea during the twenty years that it languished under multiple owners. (SG)*

Swiss that the old hotel would have to be razed, the new owners were dedicated to preserving the original structure.

But New Castle residents were wary. Speculators always seemed more interested in the great expanse of scenic Wentworth real estate than in the waning hotel. Berlinger's plans for a 550-space parking lot, 120 condominiums, and forty-eight duplex homes was immediately branded as "overdevelopment" in the tiny seaside town. Citizens who had blocked the Smiths' condo development plan in 1970 now rose in opposition to the Swiss. Publicly, the Wentworth renaissance was going full steam ahead.

The difficult summer season, though an eye-opener for the new owners, was termed successful. A team of architects, land planners, and engineers were preparing to do what Frank Jones himself had not been willing to afford—shut down completely for a one-year makeover.

A Pacific Park sales manager sent an upbeat letter to Wentworth sports enthusiasts in April 1982, filled with assurances. The swimming pool, golf course, yacht club and restaurant, tennis courts, and expanded clambake area would remain open while the hotel stayed closed all summer for reconstruction. In May, during a four-day auction, the contents of the hotel and many of its artifacts were sold off to make way for the promised renovations. Everything had to go—from bath mats to walnut Victorian bureaus. Hundreds gathered to take home a piece of the Wentworth. The hotel's freezer, for example, found its way to its sister hotel the Oceanic on Star Island, where it still operates today.

History does repeat itself when no one is watching. As John Albee had written of the original owner, Daniel Chase, in the nineteenth century, the Swiss simply "forgot to count cost," James Barker Smith told the *New Hampshire Times,* "Pacific Park maybe just underestimated the cost of year round operation. When they got into the complexity of opening the hotel year-round, they were overwhelmed."

Three more summers passed without the promised rebirth. The grande dame, locals came to realize, was actually on life support and possibly in a near-death coma. Investors were caught between the divided will of townspeople who were reluctant to

ABOVE: *A Colonial Revival column before demolition. (SG)*

OPPOSITE TOP: *A familiar New Castle sight, the hotel remained empty while owners and town residents debated its fate during the eighties and nineties. At its nadir, the hotel was used as the backdrop for a gruesome Hollywood horror film. (SG)*

OPPOSITE BOTTOM: *Paul McInnis auctions off the contents of the Wentworth in May 1982 after Pacific Park took ownership. (RMP)*

see their historic building taken down, but who were equally opposed to new housing and year-round traffic. This was to become a familiar catch-22. As in the "Bostonian" years following the death of Frank Jones, the Wentworth now moved from one corporate owner to the next. But the lessons of history were ignored; none of the owners were truly "hotel people." And with each sale, the great hotel grew smaller and its surrounding development larger.

In 1985 the General Electric Real Estate Credit Corp. assumed the debt of Pacific Park. GE discovered local opposition to the idea of razing the Wentworth and erecting a "significantly similar" hotel in its place. So a year later GE sold its interest to Great Island Trust, a group of seacoast investors, for $12.8 million. Hope springs eternal and, for a short while, preservationists clung to the belief that this partnership of local owners might restore the hotel to a "smaller first-class facility." That, at least, was what the Great Island Trust brochure promised, along with plans for 156 single-family homes on 247 Wentworth by the Sea acres. But scarcely two months later the new owners informed the press that not one of a dozen hotel operators contacted was interested in taking on the old Victorian. Sadly, and with no pun intended, Great Island said, the hotel might have to be destroyed as a "last resort."

In 1986, fading from the ravages of cancer in his home just across Little Harbor, Jim Smith told a local reporter that his beloved Wentworth now looked "like a 100-year old person with a terminal illness."

Harsh New England winters of ice and salt and wind were taking their toll. Without maintenance, the hotel was already on its way to ruin. Paint curled from the hulking white exterior plastered with No Trespassing signs. Some windows were boarded up; curtains still waved from the upper floors. The interior of the Colonial wing remained eerily resplendent with its bold columns decorated in gold leaf and carved rosettes. Videographer Hank Madden, hired to document the declining property for its owners, described the scene this way: "There are chandeliers down, water dripping, fixtures missing, and raccoons living in some of the deserted rooms."

The triage really began with the arrival of the Henley Corporation, the fourth owner in seven frustrating years. At first there were stirring signs that the ancient Victorian might again revive. Henley, with its world corporate headquarters set in nearby Hampton, had deeper pockets than Great Island Trust, which passed on twenty-one partially completed condominiums in the deal. Henley architects said the unsold high-ticket development, dubbed Club 21, had to be redesigned to attract wealthy buyers. Then the Henley Group, a holding company for technology-based companies, laid out its plans to New Castle residents in an elaborate slide show. Plans included a 170-slip marina, 156 new housing units, and nine hundred underground parking spots in an exclusive country club setting.

It was déjà vu for townspeople who had heard it all before. Many in the community of fewer than nine hundred voters still feared that the influx of so many people might overburden New Castle's one tiny grammar school, corrupt its roads and bridges, swarm its small beach and public areas, and tax sewer and water systems. Henley owners quickly took the pledge to preserve the Wentworth, or at least the oldest portion of it. Yet between the lines, there was reason for concern. Initial comments to the Herald by a corporate spokesman were less than definitive. "We intend to manage the development of the property so that its unique value can be realized for the benefit of the community and our shareholders," he said.

A slick oversized real estate brochure whispered about the historic past while the headlines read: "No longer a place to visit, It's now a place to live."

Among the most powerful enemies of the hotel at the time was former editor Ray Brighton himself. The author of local history books and newspaper columns, Brighton had not only written a biography of Frank Jones, but had also recently typed a 264-page history of the Wentworth Hotel while it was under the ownership of the Great Island Trust. In the strongest language yet seen, Brighton wrote a letter to the *Portsmouth Herald*, of which he had been editor. It read in part:

Out there in Cloud Heaven are misty-eyed zealots who believe, or so they say, that the old wooden pile should be preserved for the Second Coming. It's enough to make me barf right out in public.

The present structure, a feeble, weather-beaten remnant, is a disgrace, not only to Frank Jones, the man who built it, but also to the community that refused to let it go.

So locals watched apprehensively in 1989 as Henley Properties bulldozed eighty-five percent of the "newer" buildings and gutted even the early portion of the hotel down to its wooden studs. Meanwhile, James Barker Smith had moved to the Wentworth Home, a nursing facility in Portsmouth. Eulogized as a "Gatsbyesque" figure, he died quietly in the summer of 1990 while the hotel controversy raged on.

A year later Wentworth by the Sea all but flatlined when Henley officials applied to the town and received a permit to demolish the last surviving portion of the hotel. The alarm went out across the little seacoast like an air raid siren when a *Boston Globe* headline announced, "Wentworth by the Sea faces wrecker's ball." Watchdog reporter Clare Kittredge drove home the message that all but one of the six-member decision-makers at Henley Properties were not Seacoast locals at all, but instead lived in New York and California.

The first public figure to get involved was Joe Sawtelle, a well-known local developer and philanthropist from New Castle. Sawtelle personally stood in front of the town post office collecting signatures. Fully half the residents of Great Island signed his petition asking town officials not to issue the demolition permit to Henley. Even though he knew the citizens had no legal right to block the demolition, Sawtelle told everyone who would listen, "We can't let this happen."

"Why is this happening?" cried local historian Dorothy Vaughan, born in 1904. "There's history we can't ignore here!" New Hampshire Senator Burt Cohen warned the current owners at a crowded New Castle town meeting. "It's an incredibly significant hotel and site and people really care about it," State Representative Martha Fuller Clark told the *Globe*.

Henley corporate spokesman Walter Mountford, according to news reports, seemed unable to quell the rising protest. Even the *New Hampshire Business Review* was less than kind in its

SEQUENCE: *Small details of the deteriorating Victorian hotel attracted many artists. The images in this chapter are by Stephen Gianotti and Tom McCarron. For months prior to the sale to Ocean Properties, Gianotti had a key to the hotel and was allowed to wander the grounds taking pictures. (SG)*

coverage of a meeting in which Henley defended its actions. Mountford, according to the *Review,* "managed to antagonize most, if not all, of the New Castle residents at the meeting with a presentation that was both condescending and whiny."

The firestorm of pent-up reaction from the community over the demolition permit bought a six-month reprieve from Henley managers, who agreed not to pull the plug on the hotel until June 1992. But the situation, they admonished, was grim. The bottom had fallen out of the resort market, just as Jim Smith had predicted two decades before. The six-month New Hampshire tourist season just wasn't viable, and there was a recession. Worst of all, Henley officials implied, the ravaged remaining chunk of the hotel was an eyesore. Buyers were unwilling to pay $500,000 to a million dollars for a home within view of what Kittredge described as "a spectacle of neglect."

Michael Dingman, CEO of the Signal Capital Corporation, which included the Henley Group, sent a plea to New Castle residents on his personal stationery. He detailed the economic plight his company faced and why the hotel had to go. The letter read in part:

> The Wentworth is the image of the neighborhood and must be enhanced or removed. We have paid dearly to maintain a relic of yesteryear. The time has come to face reality and look ahead together.

A *Boston Globe* editor issued a call to arms: "Clearly some sort of cavalry headed by a modern Teddy Roosevelt needs to come over the horizon at a gallop to save Wentworth by the Sea."

The cavalry was already assembling. With the speed of a Revolutionary New England militia, New Castle residents responded to the Henley challenge. The nonprofit Friends of the Wentworth began as a painting party. A fresh coat of paint, Henley officials said, would cost $50,000 and give the building more eye appeal for future condo buyers. So forty-five initial members of the Friends set out to raise the funds to paint the Wentworth.

At Sawtelle's request, Etoile Holzaepfel, a landscape architect and New Castle resident, took on the leadership of what she imagined to be a short-term community-action project. Described by one reporter as "strong willed and pleasantly immovable," Holzaepfel took on the voluntary jobs when her daughter was in grammar school.

"I never dreamed that she would be out of college by the time the Wentworth finally opened," Holzaepfel says today. "It was a good thing we couldn't see the incredible amount of work that lay ahead back in 1991."

From the very outset, the Friends were no ordinary preservationist group. Members were driven to save the historic hotel, but not blind to fiscal reality. "We are not interested in preserving it as a relic or as a museum," Holzaepfel immediately told reporters. "Use it or lose it" was effectively the group's motto.

Although as many as seven hundred people eventually joined the cause, the Friends primarily represented New Castle residents. Within hours of the first meeting, Holzaepfel told *Preservation* magazine that the Wentworth Hotel problem, and the regulatory powers to solve the problem, were centered inside the town borders of New Castle. In three months the Friends had raised $27,000 in contributions to paint the hotel. Before the Henley deadline arrived, they had $70,000, nearly half again the targeted goal.

Local writers continued to spread the Friends' story to an ever-widening audience. It played well in the media as a tale of grassroots activism in a tiny Yankee town. In 1974, a few hundred voters in nearby Durham had crushed attempts by Greek tycoon Aristotle Onassis to build an oil refinery on New Hampshire's tiny delicate coastline. Now seacoast citizens rallied to protect a withering wooden structure from corporate developers.

Freelancer Leslie Smith, who also covered the story for the *New York Times,* offered an insightful commentary in *Seacoast Sunday,* one of many vital but short-lived local newspapers that thrived before the Internet era:

> If the Friends do rescue the Wentworth, it won't be because the old hotel evokes nostalgia for a bygone era of Victorian carriages and leghorn bonnets and smoking oil lamps. The Wentworth will stand because it

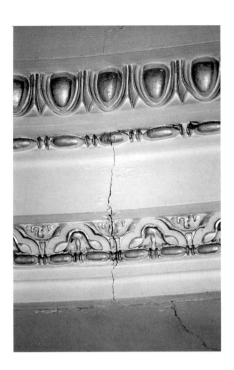

forms the nexus of shared memories that the living want to keep and cherish.

The Friends of the Wentworth brought more than money to the negotiating table. The group also assembled a detailed plan for "a smaller viable hotel" based on the research of professional consultants.

Then suddenly the players changed again. A month before the demolition deadline, Henley hired the Green Company of Newton, Massachusetts, to manage the hotel and its surrounding properties. The Friends approached the Green Company, "with paintbrushes in hand," but were told to hold off. The "Greens" were busy marketing the unsold Duck's Head condos and had their own plan for a smaller, 106-room hotel. The plan, which the town approved, also called for 129 new homes, including the demolition of the cottages on Campbell's Island. Amid the sea of change, Henley of New Hampshire announced that the company had been renamed; it was now the Koll Real Estate Group of California.

As the Wentworth languished, the Green Company pressed ahead. In 1993, acting for Koll, they sold the golf course to local owners for $3 million. By 1994 the economy was on the mend and they finally sold all of the Duck's Head condos for an average of $500,000 apiece and had begun a new cluster of luxury houses on the old hotel property. The marina, too, would eventually be sold to local investors. Frank Jones's exclusive summer playground was being drawn and quartered.

According to the buzz, Tyco International, of nearby Exeter, New Hampshire, was considering the Wentworth for its new headquarters. Among the Top 10 corporate giants in the Fortune 500 rating, Tyco was a well-respected company, still a decade away from its now infamous corporate spending scandal. But Tyco backed off and Koll gave up once again on the pesky hotel. In June Koll again called for the Wentworth to be demolished "immediately, if not sooner."

The preservationist alarm sounded again and the Friends of the Wentworth met quickly with Green Company owner Alan Green, who granted another extension. The grande dame had until October 1996. This time, however, a coat of paint was not enough. The hotel could be saved, everyone agreed, only if a legitimate buyer could be found to renovate it and run it profitably. Although there was no chance the building could ever become a hotel again, a Green Company spokesman told the *Hampton Union,* the Friends were invited to attempt to find a buyer. Late in 1995, as Margaret Smith passed away in a Georgia nursing home, the Green Company purchased the surviving portions of the Wentworth real estate from Koll and became the next official owner.

The beach sand in the hourglass was running out, but the Friends had a new strategy. Using the funds originally raised to paint the hotel, they hired Albert Rex, a graduate of Boston University, as executive director of the nonprofit agency. As the group's only paid staff member, Rex was able to devote full time to publicizing the hotel's dilemma and searching for a willing new owner.

As the June demolition deadline arrived, the Friends announced that Wentworth by the Sea had been named one of America's eleven most endangered historic places by the National Trust for Historic Preservation. This was big news. Although the trust endorsement carried no federal protection, it turned the national spotlight directly on New Castle and earned the hotel another few months of life support. *Smithsonian* magazine and the History Channel featured the endangered properties for an enormous new audience. The Wentworth was now teamed with the Pennsylvania steam railroad, Chicago's uptown theater district, rare adobe churches of New Mexico, and Little Rock High School, a civil rights shrine.

Under the warm glow of the national media, even the Green Company offered kudos to the never-say-die nonprofit group and edged away from talk of imminent demolition. "There has never been a situation where we had bulldozers lined up," a spokesman told the *Herald.* The offer on the table was for the hotel and four surrounding acres, reduced from what had been more than 250 acres. The asking price was $1 million, less than the cost of some of the luxurious condos still under construction nearby.

But the hotel with scarcely a pulse was no more than a shell of its former self. Retired Wentworth tennis pro Wadleigh Woods,

now in his nineties, told friends that when he visited the ruined old hotel, he wept. Former guests, seacoast residents, visiting Japanese tourists, and past employees did the same. People who had never known the hotel in its heyday, even those who would have been locked out of its exclusive doors, felt the loss. Broken and reduced, the hotel was no longer simply an icon of social excess or of a largely forgotten peace. The once aristocratic Wentworth now had a humbler role. It was a survivor, the last of its kind. When it fell, one more unique touchstone to the past would be gone. When people could no longer stand inside its fragile frame, one more speaking tube to the past would disappear.

Bob Devore, a former Henley executive who became a leader of the Friends of the Wentworth, continued to have faith. DeVore's parents had stayed at the Wentworth in the 1950s while he was a student at Phillips Exeter Academy. He had "owned" the Wentworth for a moment in time, and wandered its ghostly halls. Now, when only the last rites seemed inevitable, DeVore and the Friends continued to say, "We can save the Wentworth. It has that magic to it."

Then suddenly, as if channeling a thousand voices, the grande dame stirred. On February 19, 1997 the *Portsmouth Herald* ran a banner headline—"The Wentworth Is Saved." Ocean Properties, one of the nation's largest hotel management companies, had agreed, conditionally, to buy the hotel from the Green Company. In fact, Ocean Properties, headquartered right in Portsmouth, had been mulling over the purchase for a year. Company CEO Billy Walsh announced categorically to the press, "We are not going to tear that building down." The Greens gave Ocean Properties six months to make good on the sale of the Wentworth or the wrecking ball would swing.

But the extension passed without a decision. A small but influential and vocal band of townspeople was strongly opposed to the return of the hotel under any conditions. Some detractors had deep roots on Great Island; others had recently moved into new luxury homes on the old hotel grounds. A full year later, in February 1998, the Green Company issued a third extension and Ocean Properties presented its redevelopment plan to the citizens of New Castle. The endgame, everyone instinctively understood, was in play and the home court had the advantage. The plan was to incorporate the surviving structure into a modern 160-room hotel and spa, expand the building in both directions, and build eighteen hotel apartments on the site of Harry Beckwith's old Ship. Thirteen zoning changes were required for Ocean Properties to move forward. Out of 796 registered New Castle voters, five hundred attended the meeting—and passed all thirteen zoning ordinances by at least a two-to-one margin.

And still the project foundered. Frustrated by local roadblocks to construction, Ocean Properties threw in the towel in October and asked the Green Company to return its down payment on the hotel. But by December, with the continued efforts of the Friends of the Wentworth, talks were on again and the Portsmouth hotel management company received its seventh purchase extension. Close the deal by June 30, 1999, frustrated Green Company officials said firmly, or all bets are off. Betting, as it turned out, was a crisis still to come.

As the millennium approached, members of the Wentworth Homeowners Association were up in arms. A group of residents on land abutting the hotel threatened to take the Green Company to court over fears that the new hotel might offer gambling. The group wanted iron clad assurances that, even if the state and town someday made gambling legal, hotel owners would never turn the Wentworth into a casino.

All the same, late in July, Ocean Properties paid $2.25 million and became the sixth owner of the hotel since the doors had closed back during the presidency of Ronald Reagan. It was "A grand rebirth for battered old lady" the *Herald* headline declared. Though not fully revived, the grande dame was certainly showing signs of life. The State of New Hampshire, under its first female governor, Jeanne Shaheen, had agreed to pick up the cost to reroute Route 1B around the back of the hotel as Ocean Properties designers had planned. In addition, the company was set to receive federal loan assurances for $12.2 million, nearly half of the planned $25 million renovation costs. Ocean Properties owners predicted a fifteen-month building cycle and a 2001 grand opening. Owner Bill Walsh and Friends of the

Wentworth Director Etoile Holzaepfel both went on the record with their beliefs that, finally, things were looking hopeful.

Even in ruins, Wentworth by the Sea attracted movie stars. Renamed the Carleton Hotel, the building appeared briefly as a backdrop in the 1999 horror film *In Dreams*, starring Annette Bening and Robert Downey Jr. No longer the playground of the rich, the Wentworth had become the creepy setting for a Hollywood thriller. In one gruesome scene, actor Aidan Quinn wanders the abandoned hotel grounds, enters the empty structure, is murdered, and then is devoured by a starving dog. It was not the hotel's finest hour.

In November 2000 residents attending a planning board meeting broke into applause when Ocean Properties construction plans were okayed—and still the waiting game continued. On April 1, the *Portsmouth Herald* boldly announced that construction on Wentworth by the Sea had begun at long last. But the headline was only an April Fool's joke.

ABOVE: *Most of the hotel was eventually razed, leaving only the earliest structures. Roughly three hundred original acres were reduced to four acres in the final sale. (SG)*

In July 2001 something did happen. Ocean Properties demolished the Ship to make way for a cluster of extended-stay residences. It was the last act of destruction before renewal could begin. One month later, hopeful that the grande dame was indeed about to shake off her long deep sleep, Wadleigh Woods died in his Portsmouth home at the age of ninety-six. It was still another year before the new Wentworth Road was in place on the Little Harbor side of the hotel. Large numbers of workers appeared on the scene and each month more. Construction increased exponentially until it reached a fever pitch in early May 2003. With the first guests arriving in three weeks, 150 workers focused on their tasks. A million dollars' worth of windows, thirteen hundred in all, were ordered. Heated marble bathroom floors, a grand gourmet kitchen, miles of carpeting began to arrive. High-speed Internet cables sprouted from every room.

Frank Jones, who introduced steam elevators, electric lights, and the first flush toilets, would have been delighted. He might have recognized his favorite carved fireplace, now restored, and the familiar shape of the lobby and the early ballroom. He certainly would smile to see his domed parlor ceiling, trimmed in gold and decorated with the same painted cherubs against a painted blue sky. Upstairs from any window the view is all but unchanged since Victorian days. The rocky shoals are there, the old lighthouses, the expanse of Great Island with its village and fort, the city of Portsmouth, the view of the White Mountains on a clear day. Looking off toward Little Harbor, beyond where President Roosevelt moored his sailboat, a viewer can spy Governor Wentworth's ancient mansion—still remembered, still standing.

ABOVE: *Étoile Holzaepfel of Friends of the Wentworth. (EH)*

# HOTEL FORWARD

W hat a great day!" Wendy Nicholas announced with undisguised joy. "What a great day!" Nicholas, a director of the National Trust for Historic Preservation, addressed two hundred VIP guests who clustered around the portico outside the newly opened hotel on June 19, 2003. Former New Hampshire governor Jeanne Shaheen and Japanese Consul General Masuo Nishibayashi were among the dignitaries who stood with hotel owners Michael and Billy Walsh for the ribbon cutting. In a quick motion, with reenactors dressed like Teddy Roosevelt and Baron Komura to assist, Wentworth by the Sea was officially reborn.

"Today we are all friends of the Wentworth," said Etoile Holzaepfel, pausing to wipe away a tear.

Guests had begun arriving a month earlier, vying to be among the first to sleep in the Wentworth in twenty years. Their emotion, to those unfamiliar with the hotel's harrowing story, might have appeared extreme. Visitors came clutching hotel souvenirs—commemorative plates, early brochures, silver spoons, bingo cards, and photographs—passed down from family members. They traded old stories with young hotel employees. They wandered the restored rooms and familiar New Castle haunts, remembering, like alumni at a reunion.

The reanimation of the Wentworth and its stories, as one visitor observed, is more salvation than preservation. Most of the building is new, attached to either side of the original

OPPOSITE: *Aerial view of the Wentworth by the Sea Marriott Hotel and Spa opened in Spring 2003. (OP)*

nineteenth-century structure. A modern conference center looks west toward Campbell's Island. A state-of-the-art spa points east.

Wentworth by the Sea architect John Merkle, of TMS Architects, remembers the complex union of nineteenth-, twentieth-, and twenty-first-century structures. The hotel had been constantly remodeled for more than a century, he says. Load-bearing beams had been severed, spliced, severed again. Water and ice, time and neglect had taken a fearsome toll. The once rock-solid structure was, indeed, endangered, and the renovation had begun in the nick of time.

"It was only a matter of years," Merkle says. "The hotel had maybe two, maybe three years of life left. It was very close."

In retrospect, owner Billy Walsh, of Ocean Properties, is amazed so many pieces came together so smoothly. The odds, he admits, were not always in their favor. Turning a defunct Victorian summer resort into a vital year-round conference center was a challenge from the outset. Walsh says he made a list of hurdles to jump before giving the project a green light. There were issues of water, sewer, building elevation, design parameters, safety codes, variances, land use, and concerned neighbors.

"We made a list of sixty-three problems that had to be overcome," he says. "If we didn't solve them all, we could not go forward. The first thing on the list was: We have to move that road."

And the road was moved. The state of New Hampshire relocated a half mile of scenic Route 1B, bending it around the back of the hotel. Guests would never again have to dodge traffic to reach the hotel swimming pool.

If the final construction seemed frenetic to seacoast residents, it was business as usual for the Walsh family, who own or manage a hundred hotels across the country. In the last three weeks of construction, a thousand skilled workers were on the payroll.

"At one point I said, 'This one is going to be very tight,' " Michael Walsh remembers telling his brother Billy, who was working with the crew and staff trainees until two and three o'clock each morning as the grand opening day loomed.

Always, the Walsh brothers agree, there was something special about the Wentworth. It was like no other hotel in no

other community. The people, the entire seacoast, seemed to be rooting for their success. Vendors and workers offered to lend a hand on Sundays, at no extra charge.

"The Wentworth has a place in everybody's heart," Michael says. "It has a place deep in their memories. It has for us too. My aunt and uncle used to come here every year for their anniversary."

Even before the hotel opened, staff members had booked weddings to near capacity two years ahead. National media from the *Boston Globe* and *USA Today* to the *New York Times* were quick to sing the praises of New Hampshire's only grand seaside resort. By midsummer it was as if the twenty limbo years had all been a dream. Wentworth by the Sea was back.

In the end, Billy Walsh admits, it was a project too challenging to pass up. His office in Portsmouth is just a few miles away, around the historic New Castle loop. He says the constant efforts of the Friends of the Wentworth had a powerful impact on his decision, as did the support of the community, as well as the voice of his wife telling him every night—you can't quit.

It was a hotel with a name, he says. It was a hotel with a name, a history, and an irreplaceable view. It was a hotel that wanted to stay alive.

In November 2003, as the Wentworth faced its first winter season in 130 years, the Friends of the Wentworth gathered in the grand ballroom to say farewell. It was time, they all agreed, for their little nonprofit agency to ride quietly into the sunset. Their job was done.

Among the special guests, Isabel Beckwith Closson, aged ninety-seven, was telling stories of the good old days. Her father, Harry Beckwith, had owned the hotel during the roaring twenties and the Great Depression. As she spoke, her son Addison Closson Jr. settled down at the grand piano in the Roosevelt room across from Frank Jones's restored fireplace and filled the ancient hall with song. Another woman, a descendant of Charles E. Campbell, wandered from the busy gathering down the long corridor to the far end of the hotel, the sounds of the piano and conversation fading. She stood and watched in silence as the last rays of the orange sun washed over her great-grandfather's tiny island.

OPPOSITE: *The domed ceiling created in the Frank Jones' era arches over the new dining room. (OP)*

# Photo Credit Abbreviations

ATH    Portsmouth Athenaeum
BS     Bolling Smith private collection
BD     Brian DiMambro private collection
CAM    Cambell family private collection. Thanks especially to BJ
       Plantero and Alice Wentworth
DA     Douglas Armsden Photography. Many of the Portsmouth
       Athenaeum photographs originated with Douglas Armsden
       but were generously donated to the library
EH     Etoile Holzaepfel
FC     Frank Clarkson Photography
FD     Frank Daggett
FG     Frank Graham private collection
FOS    Fosters Daily Democrat, Mike Ross
HL     Harry Lichtman Photography, Newmarket NH
JA     John Albee's *New Castle Historic and Picturesque*
JDR    J. Dennis Robinson
LIB    Library of Congress
LK     Lewis Karabatsis private collection
MT     Matthew Thomas prviate collection
NEH    Norman E. Hope private collection
NHHS   New Hampshire Historical Society
OP     Ocean Properties Ltd.
PER    Peter E. Randall
PM     Patrick McSherry
PPL    Portsmouth Public Library
RHS    Rollinsford Historical Society
RMC    Richard M. Candee private collection
RMP    Ralph Morang Photography, Berwick, Maine
SG     Stephan Gianotti and Tom McCarron
SN     Seacoast Newspapers
SSC    Seacoast Science Center
UNH    University of New Hampshire publication *A Stern and
       Lovely Scene*
WJ     William A. Jewett private collection
YAN    Matthew R. Thompson

# ſelected Bibliography

Albee, John. *New Castle, Historic and Picturesque*. Boston, 1884. Reprinted Portsmouth, NH: Peter E. Randall Publisher, 1974.

Ballingall, H.M.S. "Mr. and Mrs. Smith and the Gala Days of the Wentworth by the Sea." *New Hampshire Profiles*, May 1986.

Baker, Emerson. "Lithobolia: The Rock-Throwing Devil." Lecture to the Old Berwick Historical Society, Spring 2003.

Brewster, Charles. *Rambles Around Portsmouth*. Somersworth: New Hampshire Publishing Company and Theatre by the Sea, 1972.

Brighton, Ray. *Frank Jones: King of the Alemakers*. Portsmouth, NH: Peter E. Randall Publisher, 1976.

Brighton, Ray. *The Wentworth-by-the-Sea: One of the Grand Hotels*. Portsmouth, NH: Unpublished manuscript for Great Island Trust. Portsmouth Athenaeum, 1987.

Brighton, Ray. "The Wentworth's Buried Treasure." *Rambles About Portsmouth*, Portsmouth, NH: Portsmouth Marine Society, 1994.

Burke, Maryellen, "Capsule History of Wentworth by the Sea." Friends of the Wentworth Collection. Portsmouth, NH: Portsmouth Athenaeum, 1997.

*Campbell Family Collection*. Private collection of Alice Wentworth and B.J. Plantero. Portsmouth, and Barrington, NH.

Candee, Richard M. *Building Portsmouth*. Portsmouth, NH: Portsmouth Advocates, 1992.

——. "The Wentworth-by-the-Sea: Historic Character, Preservation and New Design." Portsmouth, NH: Unpublished report with Adams & Roy Consultants, 1987.

——. *Wentworth by the Sea: Research files*. York, Maine: Private Collection.

——. *Atlantic Heights: A World War 1 Shipbuilders Community*. Portsmouth, NH: Portsmouth Marine Society, 1985.

Cash, Kevin. *Who the Hell is William Loeb?* Manchester, NH: Amoskeag Press, 1975.

Cunningham, Valerie and Mark Sammons. *Portsmouth Black Heritage Trail Resource Book*. Portsmouth, NH: Strawbery Banke Museum, 1998.

Day, Pat. "Growing Up with the Wentworth," series of articles. *Publik Occurences*, Sept. 27, Oct. 4, and Oct. 25, 1985.

Deroy, Sherry L. "Can the Wentworth be Saved?" *Business NH Magazine*, September 1996.

Doleac, Charles. Personal interview. May 2003.

Drew, William. *New Castle Walkabout: Historical Background on Old New Castle Houses*. New Castle, NH: Grist Mill Publishing, 1993.

Fardlemann, Charlotte. "Gardening Through the Years." *Women for Women Weekly*, March 18, 1980.

*Friends of the Wentworth Collection*. (Includes early hotel brochures, images, documents, hotel logs and letters.) Portsmouth, NH: Portsmouth Athenaeum, 1997.

Garvin, James L., "The Wentworth Houses of Portsmouth and Those Who Lived in Them." *Report for New Hampshire Division of Historical Resources*, October 1996.

Hepburn, Andrew. *Great Resorts of North America*. New York: Doubleday, 1965.

"The Historic Wentworth, On the Rock-Ribbed Coast of New England." *Footwear Fashion*, Aug. 1931.

*Jewett Genealogy Collection*. Private collection, McLean Virginia.

Kittredge, Clare. "The Wentworth Hotel" articles. *Boston Globe*, Nov. 10, 1991.

Lacks, Stanley B. *Going South for the Winter*. South Weymouth, MA: Unpublished Memoir, 2002.

Longfellow, Henry Wadsworth. "Lady Wentworth." *Tales of a Wayside Inn*. Boston: Houghton Mifflin, 1906.

Melanson, Susan Chapman. *Wentworth by the Sea 1969, A Novel*. Xlibris Corporation, 2000.

Miller, Leslie. "Wentworth-by-the-Sea." *Seacoast Sunday*, May 31, 1992.

Morrill, Richard. "Wentworth Never Helped New Castle People Much." *Portsmouth Herald*, Feb. 8, 1998.

"New Castle," *Granite State Monthly*, July 1880.

Perry, Nora. "Lady Wentworth." *The Galaxy*, Jan.-June 1875.

Potter, Jean. "Letter Recounting the Integration of the Wentworth by the Sea by the NAACP." Private collection, Jan. 12, 2003.

Randall, Peter E. *There Are No Victors Here: A Local Perspective on the Treaty of Portsmouth*. Portsmouth, NH: Portsmouth Marine Society, 1990.

Smith, James Barker. "Jim Smith, Hotel Entrepreneur: A Biography." Transcribed by Wadleigh Woods. Unpublished, 1990.

———. "A Philosophy for Today." Unpublished, n.d.

Spoffard, Harriet Prescott, et al. *Three Heroines of New England Romance*. Boston: Little Brown, 1894.

St. John, Helen. *From Mrs. Tredick's Inn: More Reminiscences of New Castle*. Portsmouth, NH: Peter E. Randall Publisher, 1987.

Thompson, Matthew R. and Ralph E. *First Yankee: The Story of New Hampshire's First Settler*. Portsmouth, NH: Piscataqua Pioneers, 1997.

Trani, Eugene P. *The Treaty of Portsmouth: An Adventure in American Diplomacy*. Kentucky: University of Kentucky Press, 1969.

Varrell, William M. *Summer By The Sea: The Golden Era of Victorian Beach Resorts*. Portsmouth, NH: Strawbery Banke Print Shop, 1972.

*Wentworth by the Sea Collection*. Vertical Newsclipping File. Portsmouth, NH: Portsmouth Athenaeum.

*Wentworth by the Sea Collection*. Vertical Newslipping File. Portsmouth, NH: Portsmouth Public Library.

"Wentworth by the Sea." *Granite Monthly*, July 1880.

"The Wentworth, New Castle, New Hampshire and Its Attractions as a Summer Resort." *White Mountain Echo*, Aug. 7, 1880.

Whittier, John Greenleaf. *The Complete Works of John Greenleaf Whittier*. Cambridge, MA: Houghton Mifflin Company, 1894.

Wilson, Thomas. Typewritten notes in Portsmouth Public Library vertical file. n.d.

Winslow, Richard E. III. *'Do Your Job': An Illustrated Bicentennial History of the Portsmouth Naval Shipyard, 1800-2000*. Portsmouth, NH: Portsmouth Marine Society, 2000.

——. "Frank Jones of New Hampshire: A Capitalist and a Politician During the Golden Age." Unpublished thesis. Portsmouth Public Library.

Withey, William H. *The Rockingham: The House that Jones Built*. Portsmouth, NH: Rockingham Condominium Association, 1985.

Woods, Wadleigh. "The James Barker Smiths." Unpublished, 1990.

Young, Philip. *Revolutionary Ladies*. New York: Alfred A. Knopf, 1977.

## Multimedia and Ephemera

"America's Most Endangered." History Channel segment on the National Trust's Eleven Most Endangered Sites of 1996.

Doleac, Charles, editor. Portsmouth Peace Treaty. Web site: www.portsmouthpeacetreaty.com

*Gold Diggers of 1933*. Dir. Bussby Berkeley. MGM/UA Home Video, United Artists Associates Inc., renewed 1962, released 1933.

Karabatsis, Lewis. Hotel ephemera private collection, Rye, NH.

Ocean Properties, Portsmouth, NH. Web site: www.wentworth.com

Ocean Properties. Hotel ephemera collection, New Castle, NH.

Payette, Peter, editor. Portsmouth Forts, New Castle Forts History. Web site: www.portsmouthforts.com

Robinson, J. Dennis, editor. Wentworth by the Sea History. Web site: www.seacoastnh.com/wentbysea/

"Treaty of Portsmouth." *New Hampshire Cross Roads* segment on the ninety-eighth anniversary. Sept. 4, 2003.

# INDEX

Sagamore Hotel, 30
Sagamore House, 37*p*, 59*p*
*Sailfish, U.S.S.* (submarine), 160
sailing, 148
*Saipan, U.S.S.* (aircraft carrier), 175
Sakhelin Island, 107
Sanders, Colonel, 182
Sandy Beach, 4
Sawtelle, Joe, 199, 200
*Scarborough* (ship), 9
Sea Breeze, 30
Seacoast Science Center, 7, 7*p*
*Seacoast Sunday,* 201–202
seaplanes, 143
Seavey Island, 96*p*, 97–99
Settineri, Nino and Helen, 171*p*
Shaheen, Jeanne, 205, 209, 211*p*
Shapleigh Island, 46
Shaw, Albert H., 127, 137, 141–142
Shearer, Michael Hassel, 145
The Ship, 143*p*, 144*p*, 145–146, 148, 170*p*, 181, 207
Ship Casino, 146
Shreve, Anita, 30*p*
Sign of the Anchor, 31
Sign of the Dolphin, 32, 32*p*
Signal Capital Corporation, 200
Simpson, Charles E., 48
Sinclair House, 67*p*, 133
slot machines, 181
Smith, James Barker, 41, 50, 79, 158, 164*p*, 165–191, 165*p*, 166*p*, 169*p*, 173*p*, 176*p*, 177*p*, 178*p*, 190*p*, 193, 195, 196, 199
Smith, James Barker, Jr., 166, 168*p*, 180*p*, 181, 186, 193
Smith, John, 5
Smith, Leslie, 201–202
Smith, Margaret Chase, 183
Smith, Margaret Tasher, 41, 50, 79, 164*p*, 165–191, 165*p*, 167*p*, 168*p*, 169*p*, 173*p*, 179*p*, 190*p*, 193, 203
*Smithsonian Magazine,* 203
Smuttynose Island, 30, 36, 37*p*, 38
Smuttynose Murders, 30
Smythe Isles. *See* Isle of Shoals
social-religious clubs, 52
Society of the White Ribbon, 118–119
Sorrento, Maine, 91, 92, 97, 124

South Mill Pond, 24
Southern Shoe Wholesalers, 124
sports events, 93–94, 94*p*, 95*p*
sprinkler system, 149
*Squalus* (submarine), 160, 163*p*
*St. Louis* (cruiser), 97
stables, 67
stagecoaches, 51, 62*p*, 80*p*, 108*p*
Stanton, Frank H., 148, 150–151
Star Island, 30, 38, 39*p*
*States and Union,* 153
Statler, Elsworth Milton, 165
Stone-Throwing Devil, 32–34, 34*p*
*Story of a Bad Boy* (Aldrich), 101
Strawberry Bank, 4
Strawbery Bank Museum, 5, 25–26, 26*p*
Studebaker House, 142
submarine spotting, 138*p*, 139
Sullivan, John, 9, 45
Supreme Court, U.S., 109
Swanson, Gloria, 182
Sweepstakes Commission, 181
swimming pond, 85, 123, 128*p*, 143*p*, 145–146, 181–182

Taft, Benjamin, 80
Taft, William Howard, 131
Takahira, Kogoro, 106*p*
*Tales of a Wayside Inn* (Longfellow), 22–23
*Tallapoosa* (ship), 79–80
Tally-ho coach, 80*p*, 89, 108*p*
Talmadge, Norma, 129*p*
Tanner, Virginia, 147, 147*p*
Tarbell, Edmond C., 135
Tardiff, Olive, 158, 160
Tarkington, Booth, 157
taverns, 31–33, 31*p*, 34
taxes, 24
tea set, 53, 53*p*
telephones, 67
Temple, Shirley, 183
tennis, 70*p*, 71, 94*p*, 123, 172, 174, 174*p*
Thanksgiving, 178*p*
Thaxter, Celia, 38, 38*p*, 101
Thompson, Amais, 5
Thompson, David, 5, 7, 7*p*, 162

Thompson, George T., 81, 93
Thompson, John, 5
Thomson, David. *See* Thompson, David
Thomson, Madeline, 160
Thoreau, Henry David, 35
Thurmond, Strom, 175, 177
Tilton, Frank, 143
Tilton, John P., 142, 151–152
Tip-Top House, 35
TMS Architects, 210
Togo, Fumihiko, 119*p*
*Toucey, U.S.S.* (battleship), 155
tourism, 28*p*, 29–30, 29*p*, 35–36, 35*p*, 75–76, 200
tower, 40*p*, 47*p*, 89, 91
Towle, Loren D., 125, 127
treasure map, 86, 87, 89
Treaty of Portsmouth, 105*p*, 106*p*, 107, 107*p*, 108*p*, 109–118, 110*p*, 111*p*, 112*p*, 114*p*, 115*p*, 116*p*, 117*p*, 118*p*, 119*p*, 123, 141
Trefethen family, 43
Tripp, Stanley W., 124
trolley, 129, 131–133, 132*p*
trophies, 189*p*
Truman, Harry S, 80, 175
Tufts, Jean and Arthur, 170, 187*p*
turtle racing, 172, 188*p*
Tyco International, 202

Urch, David, 73, 131–133, 132*p*, 133

Van Horn, Welby, 174
Vaughan, Dorothy, 199

Wagner, Louis, 30
Wainwright, Helen, 147, 148*p*
The Wait-a-While, 133, 132*p*
Walbach, Colonel, 13
Walbach Tower, 12*p*, 13
Wallis Sands, 30, 133
Walsh, Billy, 204, 205, 209, 210, 210*p*, 212
Walsh, Michael, 209, 210, 212
Walton, Alice, 34
Walton, George, 31, 31*p*, 32–34, 34, 34*p*
War of 1812, 10

# ABOUT THE AUTHOR

J. Dennis Robinson is owner and editor of SeacoastNH.com, one of New England's most popular regional Web portals. A teacher, columnist, lecturer, and video producer, he has published over a thousand articles about Maine and New Hampshire history and culture. He lives in Portsmouth with his wife Maryellen.